What People Are Saying About Fancy Fast Food

"Never have so many Americans been forced to confront champagne taste with a beer budget. Now, like manna from virtual Heaven, there's a website to help you create gourmet meals (or gourmet-looking meals) from ingredients off the $1 menu."

– Jane Wells, CNBC

"Food porn begets fast food porn, which in turn has come to verge on fast food parody, some of it perhaps intentional. The website Fancy Fast Food actually devises and presents recipes for seemingly refined, accomplished dishes that just rearrange and redeploy ingredients in items purchased directly from, say, Kentucky Fried Chicken. Or Domino's. That chain's American Legends Pacific Veggie Pizza is the entirety of the shopping list for a dish that Fancy Fast Food labels Dao Mi Noh Chow Mein and that, as pictured on the site, looks like something in a proper Chinese restaurant."

– Frank Bruni, *The New York Times* Week in Review

"Fancy Fast Food makes your favorite junk into eye candy."

– Alex Chasick, The Consumerist

"Whether you're a White Castle virgin or a Burger King slut, you'll certainly be able to appreciate the artistry involved in transforming fast food meals into haute (looking) cuisine. The amazing extreme makeovers featured on Fancy Fast Food don't sound appetizing, but they sure look edible."

– Chantal Martineau, *The Village Voice*

"*Why We Love It*: It's hilarious, unique and very entertaining. [Fancy Fast Food] provides a step-by-step guide to turning fast food into a fancy dish, so it's also informative. It just proves that 'just because something looks gourmet doesn't mean it started that way'... Plus, who wouldn't want to look at fast food all day?"

– Fox News' iMag, Best Food Humor Blog

Fancy Fast Food™

Ironic Recipes with No Bun Intended

✸ ✸ ✸ ✸ ✸

Erik R. Trinidad

With Illustrations by Maurice Murdock

©2012 Erik R. Trinidad.

All rights reserved.

No part of this book may be used or reproduced, stored in a retrieval system or transmitted in any form, or by any means, electronic, mechanical, photocopied, recorded or otherwise, without written permission of the publisher except in the case of brief quotations embodied in critical articles and reviews.

Published by World Swirl Press via CreateSpace, an Amazon.com company

ISBN 978-0615570341

Photographs by Erik R. Trinidad
Illustrations by Maurice Murdock

No celebrity chefs were harmed during the creation of this book.

Note: The ingredient lists of each recipe in this book were based on available menu items at individual fast food chains at the time of creation, from May 2009 to December 2010. Participating locations may vary.

10 9 8 7 6 5 4 3 2 1

For my brother Mark

The Guy Behind The Guy

FANCY CONTENTS

Fancy Introduction, 1

Fancy Appetizers, 8
Beef C'Arbysccio • King of Quiche • Chick-Sat-A • Five Guys Foie Gras American Domplings • Tapas de Castillo Blanco

Fancy Soups & Stews, 32
Gazschlotzcho • The Colonel's Chicken Corn Chowder • Fuddjoada Whatagatawny • Moe's Southwest Cassoulet • Soniccian Borscht

Fancy Poultry, 52
Chicken, Cheddar & Mushroom Zoufflé • Le Chicken McConfit • Jack In The Bento • Coq Au Cheervin • Chicken Pizza Masala • Chicken Mole Frostano

Fancy Meats, 74
Beef Wellington, Animal Style • Carlbonade Flamande • Gras-Fed Steak Au Poivre • Wiener Schnitzel Fälschung • Beef Strog 'N Off • Whop Perguignon

Fancy Seafood, 96
Long John Ceviche • Gumbo D-Luxe • Seafood Fauxsotto
Spicy Chicken Mocki Sushi • Baja Bouillabaisse • Quenelles-O-Fish

Fancy Pasta & Noodles, 116
Tacobellini • Del Spaghetti Arrabbiata • Chinese Checkers Chow Mein
Five-Dollar Farfalle • Chicken Chipotlioli • Cheat Potato Gnocchi

Fancy Holiday Meals, 136
A Valentine's Paella Yoshinolla • Franksgiving Dinner • Bubbe Wendy's Hanukkah Latkes • Honey Apple Glazed Christmas Holiday Ham • Fondue du Sept-Onze

Fancy Desserts, 154
Boston Krème Brûlée & Fruit Tart • Culvoutis • Blizzard Blintz
Maggie Mousse • Tiramisu Di Timio

Fancy Conclusion, 172

Behind the Fancy Fast Food, 174

Acknowledgments, 178

Index, 181

Amuse your bouche on this:
Chicken Cordon Deux
(a fancy KFC Double Down)

FANCY INTRODUCTION

Fast food is *awesome.* There, I said it. While some of you may not agree, I'm guessing many others reading this do, for nothing but fast food really hits the spot, especially when you're hungry on a long road trip. But you don't have to drive that far to have the craving; even if you're home with a case of the munchies, there's just no substitute for fast food. And as for the urban myth that greasy fast food is a cure-all for the common hangover? *True.*

Let me clarify that I'm not talking about those quick and easy meals you can prepare in a jiffy; a prep time of ten minutes feels like an *eternity* when you've got stuff to do, and it takes away from all that valuable time you could spend stalking your friends on Facebook. No, I'm talking about junky fast food, the kind that comes in a box or a wrapper and is served to "billions and billions" by the dozens of fast food franchise companies out there. I won't deny that they may be partly to blame for America's obesity problem, but even if you are in shape, sometimes you just crave that crappy processed factory food flavor (because it's engineered that way). It may be true what they say in the numerous reports of fast food not being good for you, but hey, so is a pricier gourmet filet mignon loaded with truffle butter, and that's awesome too.

LOVE IT OR HATE IT, fast food is ubiquitous and is here to stay. Why? Well not only is it fast, but it's also cheap and filling. For less than eight bucks you can buy your entire calorie, sodium, or fat requirements for the day — and most likely, the rest of the week. Plus, as Morgan Spurlock pointed out in his documentary *Super Size Me,* fast food can also be nostalgic. For some, a trip to McDonald's can conjure up childhood memories of Happy Meals, birthday parties, and PlayPlaces. I know I'll never forget how fun my tenth birthday party was in a McDonald's party room fashioned to look like Hamburglar's prison cell in Hackensack, New Jersey. (I'm not kidding.) It has conditioned me to think of prison as a happy place where you can trade French fries instead of cigarettes for favors, without having to become a fellow inmate's "bitch."

Fast food is America's gastronomic guilty pleasure, and it's expanded into other countries, as I've learned on my travels around the world. Did you know there's a McDonald's tucked in a little alley in Venice? A Hooters in the neighborhood of the resting place of Eva "Evita" Perón? And a Pizza Hut across the street from the Great Sphinx and Pyramids in Egypt? They don't show you that on the Discovery Channel. Maybe it's because their shows only dramatize the "exotic" in a locale, turning a blind eye to the reality of American fast food imperialism. Not that I'm endorsing eating at American fast food joints while traveling abroad, although I do get a kick out of seeing McDonald's take on region-specific cuisine. (For example, the "McArabia" is chicken or kofta on a pita with lettuce, tomatoes, onions, and garlic mayonnaise.)

I will however say that the international presence of American fast food has actually been helpful in my days of flashpacking on the road, sampling all kinds of indigenous food; when I had an inevitable case of "Delhi belly" (aka travelers' diarrhea) in India, a strict regiment of McDonald's Chicken Maharaja-Macs for two days cleared me right up.

You can really feel the history of the pharaohs with the view from inside the Giza Pizza Hut.

ORGANIC SCHMORGANIC?

Believe the hype or not, buying "certified organic" is the better way to go when grocery shopping these days — that is, if you can afford it. If not, you'll still be okay; we've been eating nonorganic food for decades, and we're still around to tell the tale. But if you have the means, going organic can be beneficial. Without the use of harmful chemicals in food production, it's not only better for your personal health, it's better for the environment — and if the food is "grown locally," it can help reduce our monstrous size 23 carbon footprint. (Some may consider that size to be acceptable, but you know what they say about people with big footprints.*)

However, being labeled "organic" hasn't always been completely genuine over the years, since there have been many existing loopholes that could be exploited. For example, some grains could be called "organic" and still be grown with an approved list of pesticides. Loopholes can also be exploited with other greenwashing buzz words:

"Cage-Free" means that no cages are involved, but that doesn't necessarily mean there's no overcrowding under the roof of that chicken coop. To make a comparison, sure you can shove hundreds of Japanese businessmen on an already crowded Tokyo subway train, but it's still technically not a "cage." With that said, "cage-free" eggs are also "train-free" — and what's healthier than a train-free omelet?

"All-Natural" has no official definition by the FDA, which means that a granola bar can be "all natural" even if it's packed with "all-natural" high-fructose corn syrup. It might as well be labeled "somewhat ambiguous," but then again, that isn't defined either.

"Free-Range" and **"Grass-Fed"** only designate that an animal has access to the outdoors, but it doesn't necessarily mean it will actually go outside — especially when the outdoor farm experience can be simulated indoors by playing Farmville instead.

But I kid. The point I'm trying to make is just because you read the label doesn't necessarily mean that label stands for anything good. However, new government policies are being put into place with each passing month to tighten these loopholes and to ensure that you're getting what you pay extra for. So I'll reiterate: it can't hurt to buy something with the "organic" or "local" label on it, unless you can't afford it — or simply don't care. You could always just play the loophole game too and "go local" by going down to your "local" McDonald's and getting some cheap, somewhat-ambiguous food.

They have big socks.

ONLY THE FRESHEST FAST FOOD

A chef at a gourmet restaurant may go to the nearest butcher, organic grocery, or farmers market to get the freshest ingredients, but you, the Fancy Fast Food Chef, must resort to a greater, greasier food source. All of those other chefs may start with less-processed food, but hey, at least you may have the option of drive-thru window service.

Here are some tips on getting the freshest fast food money can buy:

- **Time your visit properly.** If you are getting items off the lunch/dinner menu, make sure you get there just before they swap out the breakfast menu. If you are getting breakfast items, arrive just before they open. This will help you avoid getting any food that's been sitting under a heat lamp for hours, which completely dries it out. Hockey pucks belong on the rink, not in your kitchen.

- **Empty all your French fries in a paper bag, and shake it for five seconds.** If you can see your fingers through a part of the bag that has become translucent from all the hot, moist oil, you know it came fresh from the fryer.

- When dealing with salads or sandwich fixings, **inspect the tomato slices to see if they're ripe**. This can easily be done by throwing one against a car window. A perfect tomato slice shouldn't bounce or turn into mush; it should stick to the glass and slowly slide downward. (This test is ideally performed on someone *else's* car.)

- If a pizza takes longer than thirty minutes to arrive, it's not the freshest it could be. "Every minute a pizza is out of the oven, the less fresh it becomes." **Tell that to the delivery guy when you stiff him the tip so he learns to come with a sense of urgency next time**, and then scream at him in a threatening Jack Bauer manner, "We don't have time to lose! I need that pizza *now*!!!"

- **Squeeze the buns.** If they are soft, they are most likely fresh. (If you misinterpret the "buns" in this tip for a part of the human anatomy on somebody, it is *you* who is the fresh one.)

- **If you have the option, order a burger a specific way** (i.e., add bacon, lose the tomatoes) so you know it's freshly prepared. Just don't get too picky with your customized order or you may risk a getting a loogeyburger from a disgruntled employee — or worse. (*Never* ask for extra mayonnaise.)

That's right, I just referred to Mickey D's as being *healthy* — even curing me from an ailment — but that is an anomaly. However, all of the fast food chains have recently embraced the mainstream ideal of a healthier lifestyle, for we now live in a culinary culture with movements encouraging "local," "organic," and "sustainable" products — movements I wholeheartedly support whenever I don't feel like they're ripping me off. Fast food chains are trying (or at least pretending) to improve their options for their customers, like offering more variety in salads and fruit servings. For example, Happy Meals now come with apple slices in addition to a reduced-sized portion of fries (which is fine by me, as long as I can still get a toy).

The other trend in food these days is going gourmet. More than ever, fancy restaurants are hot, and food-related television shows are in fashion, complete with all the overly dramatic characters you would expect from reality TV. Chefs, pitmasters, food critics, and even some butchers have been elevated to celebrity status; I've seen superstar celebrity chef Mario Batali's face on a huge billboard, headlining a forum at a casino. Even street food has gone gourmet; New York's Vendy Awards, honoring the best of street food fare, has transformed what started out as cheap food into an event with admission ticket prices close to $100 per person.

Frankly, I think it's gone a bit overboard. As Marie says to Jess in the classic, yuppie romantic comedy *When Harry Met Sally*, "I think restaurants have become too important... Restaurants are to people in the '80s what theater was to people in the '60s." Over two decades later it still rings true, and I couldn't agree more. Mario Batali headlining a casino show? Seriously? It wasn't too long ago that such an honor was usually only given to dated musical acts, like Huey Lewis and the News.

TIPS FROM AN EMPTY JAR

The signs in restaurant bathrooms may say, "Employees must wash hands before returning to work," but seriously, folks, everyone should; it's really not that hard.

No longer are the days of being hip to be square; it's now hip to be a "foodie," a term that some people, including yours truly, have come to resent. Originally, a foodie was an individual in a small sect of society that truly enjoyed the eating experience, but over the years it's blown up to be what chef Dale Levitski and food journalist Laurel Miller have referred to as "the new F-bomb." "Foodie" has become this somewhat pretentious term that self-righteous diners use to label themselves. "Oh, I'm *such* a foodie..." one might say before bragging about the latest to-*die*-for restaurant that you simply *must* try. "The ice water here at Restaurant A is mediocre at best. It's so much more delectable at Restaurant B... *blah blah blah*..."

Nevertheless I would be hypocritical if I said I completely hated these people; one might label me as such since I'm guilty of enjoying different kinds food and comparing restaurants, like many of you. But I'm not talking about the casual foodie; I'm referring to those zealous gourmet foodies out there, who really have no means to validate themselves without talking and/or Tweeting about food — the people who have become food snobs about every little detail, who brag about their meals at celebrity chef restaurants, who constantly take pictures of their meals for "food porn." Writer Joe Pompeo of *The New York Observer* cleverly labeled these food zealots as *"foodiots."*

FANCY INTRODUCTION

> **FAST FOOD FOR THOUGHT**
>
> *Apart from KFC's gimmicky breadless marketing campaign, the Double Down is not that different from Chicken Cordon Bleu, an established and well-respected recipe from the gourmet chefs of the famous eponymous French culinary institution. And, of course, everyone knows everything in France is fancy, especially when it's spelled and pronounced "bleu" instead of "blue."*

But food is for everyone. The reason why food is such a hot topic is because everyone on this planet needs it to survive — stockbrokers, rabbis, zookeepers, construction workers, tribesmen, web developers, truck drivers, strippers, bankers, ranch hands, satirical cookbook authors, you name it. Food is the common denominator of all humanity, and these zealous gourmet foodies have created a class structure around it, where meals can be classified as being everything from "junk food" to what the French call *haute cuisine*.

Well I am from America, Land of the Free(dom Fries), and I know that there is no caste system here. We live in a free society where anyone of any class can work his or her way up the metaphorical "food chain" — so why not our food? The fast food establishments may have made their menus healthier, but it's all still served in ugly wrappers or boxes. Why settle for junky-looking food when you can work a little kitchen magic and transform it into *haute cuisine*? Or at least make it *look* like it could be?

Welcome to **Fancy Fast Food: Ironic Recipes with No Bun Intended**. In this book, you will learn how to transform your burgers, French fries, hot dogs, burritos, fried chicken, and other processed fast food items into gourmet-looking meals that you might find at a five-star restaurant — all without adding a single outside ingredient (other than an occasional garnish). Who says a bun can't be reshaped into farfalle and hot dogs into *foie gras*? You will revert to your childhood and play with your food — but yield some great grown-up restaurant results. Impress your friends! Wow your spouse! Be the hit of every dinner party without spending a small fortune! But heed the warning: chances are it will taste exactly as it did before you dressed it up; it's all processed food anyway, and you are simply adding another process. Also, it should go without say that it will probably still be bad for you — but who cares? Check out how good it can look! *Bellissima!*

So rush off and grab something from your nearest fast food restaurant, preheat your oven, and sharpen your knives. You are about to become the fanciest gourmet chef this side of the Golden Arches. *Bon appétit!*

> **TIPS FROM AN EMPTY JAR**
>
> *When a recipe calls for a "reduction," I'm referring to the process of boiling a liquid down to a concentrate; it has nothing to do with weight loss because that's just not going to happen here — unless of course you substitute Diet Coke for regular when making a reduction to look like soy sauce or balsamic vinegar.*

THE GARNISH EXCEPTION

Sure, anyone could add outside ingredients to all this fast food to make it fancy like they do on fast food challenges on television, but where's the integrity in that? Limitations spawn creative ingenuity, which is what will separate you from that whiny chef on *Top Chef Masters* who got all dramatic when he couldn't prepare all his Whole Foods groceries in time for judging.

Each of the recipes in the following chapters doesn't call for any ingredients outside of the menu of the fast food establishment it is sourced from — not even water, unless it comes from the soda fountain, a purchased bottle, or melted ice. There's no deep frying in these recipes because no one has frying oil on the menu — and you can't really squeeze enough out of the fries. Just like in life, you've got to play with the cards you've been dealt. However, one outside ingredient is permissible — but only when the situation calls for it — in accordance to the rules I've established: *garnish*. Think about it; what can make any fancy entrée extra fancy whether it's derived from fast food or not? Garnish, of course.

A garnish of herbs or zest really gives a drab-looking dish an artistic splash of color, depth, and panache. And so, some recipes in this book call for added parsley, chives, cilantro, thyme, basil, or mint leaves. Anyone can see that merely adding a bit of green herbs on top of food makes any plate look ten times fancier — that is, everyone but an old girlfriend of mine who broke up with me partly because I once put dried chives on her Kraft Macaroni & Cheese. Granted, she was a "mac and cheese purist" and only ate her nostalgic boxed mac and cheese as is (which I can totally respect), plus the dried chives weren't nearly as pleasing as fresh ones. Consider it a lesson learned: when adding outside garnish to these Fancy Fast Food recipes, only use *fresh* herbs, organically grown if possible. This tops off your ironic *faux haute cuisine* with an extra touch of irony.

Heed this example of how green garnish ameliorates a dish's aesthetic:

Kraft Macaroni & Cheese made by using the instructions on the box looks like a mean old school lunchlady made it...

...but it looks like it might have come from a fancy restaurant chef with the simple touch of organic chives as garnish.

It takes some big cajones to make balls out of fast food.

FANCY APPETIZERS

✳ ✳ ✳ ✳ ✳

Remember when you were a kid and your mother told you not to eat those cookies before supper because they'd spoil your appetite? Well, she was obviously wrong! We all know that restaurants have an entire socially acceptable section on their menus specifically designed to do just that: *ruin your appetite*. Sure, appetizers are intended to tease your taste buds into wanting more, but in many establishments the portions are so huge that — unless you share them — they are bound to fill you up and double your dinner's calorie count. (This is especially true at the Olive Garden, where those unlimited buttery breadsticks just *won't* stop coming.)

Call it irony; appetizers *ruin* your appetite. Your mother was right. But chances are you don't care about the calorie counts — just like you didn't when you were a kid — so go ahead and get that spinach artichoke dip. Spoil your dinner. See if I care. I double dare you.

BEEF C'ARBYSCCIO

❋ ❋ ❋ ❋ ❋

For those who live life in the raw (or just fake it).

The Raw Foods Movement may be getting plenty of attention these days in our modern food-obsessed culture, but it's actually been practiced by people for millennia — from the first caveman who bit into an uncooked, prehistoric McRib before fire was invented, to celebrity raw-food-diet-endorsing Demi Moore, who has been munching on raw vegetables since before Ashton Kutcher was invented.

The fast food chains haven't really embraced raw foods (other than their salad offerings), but that doesn't mean you can't pretend things are raw. For this mock recipe, we are going to close our eyes and pretend beef is raw when making a beef *carpaccio* — and what classier place to get our freshly sliced beef than the fast food home of roast beef sandwiches.

Ingredients (from Arby's):

1 Super Roast Beef Sandwich
1 Roast Turkey and Swiss Sandwich
1 order of Jalapeño Bites
1 Side Salad
1 medium Fruit Punch
packets of Arby's Sauce and Horsey Sauce

10 FANCY APPETIZERS

First, **take apart the roast beef sandwich** and discover what we already know: that the roast beef isn't raw; it's roasted after all, and it's brown colored. Raw beef is supposed to be red, so we're going to have to dye the beef. This is where the fruit punch comes in. **Pour the fruit punch** in a nonstick skillet and **bring it to a boil** so that it starts reducing. We want the red syrupy goodness to thicken before putting in slices of the roast beef. **Coat both sides of the meat** until it soaks up the red liquid. Then place the meat on a fancy white platter.

The red syrup will almost immediately start to dry out, so use a pastry brush to **reapply the syrup** as needed. For extra redness, you can

THE FOOD MOVE

HERBIVORES

Raw Vegans

These extreme vegetarian hippie liberals are so left, they don't even cook their veggies above 115°F. They believe that cooking food burns away natural nutrients, so they eat their veggies raw — which is a pretty good idea if you're a *pet rabbit*.

Vegans

These people are just like raw vegans, only they acknowledge caveman's discovery of fire. Many of them are animal lovers and own pets that eat better than people in developing nations. Also, when they go to S&M clubs, they don't wear leather; they opt to wear dominatrix outfits made out of black organic cotton.

Vegetarians

These are pro-choice vegans who believe that a chicken's life doesn't necessarily begin before the egg is hatched. Vegetarians love salads, omelets, falafels, and Polly-O string cheese, and often dine with their nonvegetarian friends armed with the catch phrase, "I can always find something." (They usually do.)

Fake Vegetarians

These delusional people often tell people, "I'm a vegetarian, but I also eat chicken and fish." Real vegetarians hate these posers; that's like being in the KKK and voting for Obama, or claiming to be a feminist and rapping all the lyrics to "Baby Got Back" by heart.

brush on some packets of the reddish Arby's Sauce** as well.

Meanwhile, **skin the jalapeño bites**, and **slice them** length-wise into strips. Then use them to garnish the plate. While you're at the cutting board, **cut the Swiss cheese** from the turkey sandwich into smaller pieces; use this for garnish too. For added flair, **drizzle some Horsey Sauce** on top with a squeeze bottle. Finally, **top the meat** with some greens from the side salad and, if you want, **slice the bread and buns** into smaller pieces to serve it on the side. *Presto!* It's so easy, even a caveman could do it — or Demi Moore, if she ever felt like it.

MENT SPECTRUM

CARNIVORES

Lean Cuisiners

Constantly watching their weight, these types are always trying to eat healthy by doing silly things like completely cutting red meat out of their diet. They often hog up room in the office freezer with all their lunches: frozen microwaveable TV dinners with calorie counts on them.

Omnivores

These people eat it all. This sounds good on paper, but psychological studies have shown that people get indecisive when there are too many options to choose from. They are always calling their significant others to ask, "What should we have for dinner tonight?" and are in constant state of dilemma.

Texans

Texas' big size is to its surrounding states as their meat consumption is to their surrounding other food groups. When you're from big cattle country of steak and barbecue, it's always an all-out meatapalooza — unless of course you're one of those progressive, vegetable-eating hipsters in Austin.

Atkins Dieters

These fad dieters eat meat, the whole meat, and nothing but the meat — all with the unhealthy justification that it helps them lose weight. However, all the weight they lose is gained when they are forced to lug around a defibrillator everywhere.

KING OF QUICHE

✣ ✣ ✣ ✣ ✣

It's time to man up.

The often-quoted title of Bruce Ferstein's best-selling book is *Real Men Don't Eat Quiche*. Let's evaluate this: just what makes a man *real*? Is it a penchant for sports and video games? A constant yearning to quote one-liners from old Arnold Schwarzenegger action flicks? Or merely an inclination to scratch one's balls? Well, I exemplify all of those, and I'll admit, I'm quite keen on the quiche. If that ousts me from the realm of real manhood, don't worry, *I'll be bahck...*

Perhaps the sentiment is true: real manly lumberjack-types don't eat quiche. Instead they eat flapjacks, steaks, sausages, beef jerky, and plenty of other things that lead to cardiac arrest. But would the manliest man eat, or even prepare, a dainty quiche if it came from the *King of Burgers?*

Ingredients (from Burger King):

1 Croissan'wich (with ham)
1 Ham, Egg & Cheese Biscuit
2 orders of Hash Browns
1 Coffee
1 Orange Juice
1 bottle of water

Okay, manly man, **rip the two breakfast sandwiches apart** to pull out its insides: the eggs, bread, and ham. Set those innards aside as you **break apart the croissant** into smaller pieces and **put them in a food processor. Crumble the biscuit** and add it to the pile. **Pour in some water** and mix it until it is broken down to dough, then **mold it into a nonstick quiche pan** to form a crust.

Next, take all the eggs, some ham and some hash browns and **chop them in the food processor** until it's all scrambled together, and then **spoon the mix into the crusts**. Fire up the oven at 400°F and **bake it for 10 minutes**. When it's ready, take it out and let it cool.

--- TIPS FROM AN EMPTY JAR ---

For extra manly manness, prepare this entire recipe while watching football. And if your girlfriend or wife distracts you, tell her to go make you a sandwich.

KING OF QUICHE

Now brace yourself; quiche is about to become a nutritious part of this manly man's complete breakfast. **Accompany the dish with coffee** poured in a fancy espresso cup, and orange juice in a wine glass — just make sure you **don't hold either with your pinky in the air**; real men may each quiche now, but they *definitely* don't do *that*.

TIPS FROM AN EMPTY JAR

For an added touch of machismo, serve the quiche while wearing aviator sunglasses and say something bad-ass like, "I eat pieces of quiche like you for breakfast."

IS IT ME, OR DID BK'S KING LOOK LIKE A CHILD MOLESTER?

Give it to Crispin Porter + Bogusky — the ad agency behind Burger King from 2003 to 2011 — to bring back arguably one of the creepiest fast food mascots ever made. Let's face it, out of all the fast food mascots in history, the most disturbing has got to be the "king" from Burger King. Just look at him: those shiny, curly locks, that '70s pimp outfit, that porn mustache, and that incessant, pervy grin made out of cheap plastic. Seriously, with a mascot like that, why haven't Burger King locations popped up on maps of registered sex offenders? He didn't look like the king of burgers;

he looked like the king of smut. How had he not made an appearance as a "predator" in a *Dateline* segment? Adding to his creep factor is the fact that he never talked; he just stood there like he's constantly undressing you with his eyes. I'm sure if he could ever speak, he'd approach his targets with the come-on line, "Hey, so would you like to come back to my place and get a taste of my... *Whopper?*"

16 FANCY APPETIZERS

CHICK-SAT-A

✳ ✳ ✳ ✳ ✳

Sawadee, chickadees.

When you think about it, the southeast of the USA is not that different from Southeast Asia; they are both home to a people who manage to maintain a friendly disposition despite the tropical storms, the summertime heat and humidity, and the tourists who occasionally show up wearing bad cabana apparel and/or socks with their sandals. With that said, here's a little recipe that further bridges two "southeast" regions from different parts of the globe; it's a Southeast Asian treat derived from the southeastern American-based fast food chicken chain, Chick-fil-A.

It's convenient that you can make this in the sanctuary of your home, so you don't have to set foot inside one of those trendy "fusion" restaurants, or travel through the muggy conditions of those southeastern regions. (Let Anthony Bourdain sweat through the heat while you prepare this in the comfort of air-conditioning.)

**Ingredients
 (from Chick-fil-A):**

1 order of Chick-n-Strips (4)
1 order of Waffle Potato Fries
1 Carrot & Raisin Salad
1 Walnut Fudge Brownie
1 soft drink of your choice
packets of Barbecue, Polynesian,
 Buffalo, and Honey Mustard
 Sauce

PLUS: a banana leaf
 (for presentation)

First, **skin the breading off the Chick-n-Strips** to expose the breast meat within. **Rinse the chicken pieces** in a colander and then **cut them down** into eight bite-sized pieces. These pieces are already cooked and ready to eat, but with Fancy Fast Food, it's all about looks — so we'll make some grill marks in the manner many fast food places do: by faking it.

> **TIPS FROM AN EMPTY JAR**
>
> *Chick-fil-A's corporate headquarters is run by devout evangelical Christians. If the power of Christ compels you, rinse the chicken pieces in holy water and pray for their sins.*

Take each piece of chicken and **carve two parallel lines** in each of the sides. These double lines will help define the grill marks when you use a kitchen torch to **burn in the two dark markings** manually. Afterwards, let the chicken cool down and then **thread them onto bamboo skewers**.

Satay is typically served with a peanut sauce, but the only nuts you'll see at Chick-fil-A (other than perhaps some religious ones) are the walnuts in the walnut fudge brownie. So **pick all the walnuts off the brownie**, and then **chop them finely** with a knife. **Mix the nuts** in a small bowl and then **add in the dipping sauces** until it takes on an authentic peanut satay sauce hue.

Finally, plate your meal: **cut the banana leaf** to the size and shape of a fancy platter, and place it on top of the plate. Next, **place the little bowl of sauce and the chicken skewers**,

and then **garnish it** with a waffle potato fry and some carrot and raisin salad. **Serve with your beverage** in a nice glass, topped off with a little cocktail umbrella. And there you have it: a fancy Southeast Asian dish by means of southeastern America, and all without leaving the house.

FAST FOOD FOR THOUGHT

Y or N? If you swap the "y" for "n," you have "satan" sauce instead of "satay" sauce. Well, isn't that special?

THE MULTI-PURPOSE KITCHEN TORCH

The kitchen torch is one of my favorite kitchen gadgets. I mean, what's not to like about getting to play with a *miniature flamethrower?* If that doesn't satisfy the inner pyromaniac in all of us in a conveniently controlled manner, I don't know what does.

Still feeling a little pyro after preparing this recipe? Here are some other excuses to play with your kitchen torch when you're not faking grill marks on a fancy fake chicken satay:

- fake grill marks on burgers
- fake grill marks on hot dogs
- make a grilled cheese sandwich (the hard way)
- set off illegal fireworks
- burn an image of the Virgin Mary into a piece of toast and try and pass it off as a miracle
- start a campfire
- light birthday candles — until they're completely melted

20 FANCY APPETIZERS

FIVE GUYS FOIE GRAS

✳ ✳ ✳ ✳ ✳

It's only a wild goose chase if geese are involved.

Foie gras, which translates from French as "fat liver," is that deliciously rich and mushy delicacy that has been a proud culinary tradition of the French for centuries. Derived from the organs of ducks and geese, the "fat" in the liver comes from the fact that these members of the poultry family are traditionally force-fed tons of starch so that their livers balloon up like bratty girls who chew on experimental gum inside Willy Wonka's Chocolate Factory.

Naturally, the force-feeding of animals isn't quite well-received these days; centuries of French gastronomic heritage are no match for today's ethically conscious world of animal rights activists, who police meat-eaters like a bunch of Oompa-Loompas. The force-feeding of these birds is considered cruel and inhumane, even if they are decapitated and slaughtered for their meat anyway. Now I certainly don't want to piss off any goose-loving PETA readers out there with this recipe, so let's play with some slaughtered cows instead. (They'll hate me for that anyway, but at least beef is cheaper.)

**Ingredients
  (from Five Guys):**

5 Hamburgers with onions, lettuce, tomatoes, mushrooms, green peppers, and pickles
5–6 condiment cups of mustard
various condiments of your liking
  (i.e., relish)
salt and pepper packets
1 medium cup of water

TIPS FROM AN EMPTY JAR

It's best to deal with the non-animal ingredients first; they don't have souls and couldn't care less if we murdered them.

First, **take out all the vegetable toppings** and divide them onto separate plates so that you don't have to sort through them later. **Chop each of them down** so you can use them as a garnish for when we plate the *faux foie gras* as *hors d'oeuvres*. As for the buns, **place them on a baking sheet** and **toast them in a preheated oven** for 5–10 minutes at 400°F until they become warm and crusty.

Take the hamburger patties — there are two in each burger — and **stick them in a food processor**. Add a little water, **push the chop button**, and let it transform back into a pasty ground beef. (Hear that? Not a peep of torment from those burgers.) **Process as many patties that will fit at a time**, depending on the capacity of your appliance. Once all the beef has been ground, **transfer it into a big mixing bowl** and **fold in all the mustard** so that our mixture looks a little more yellow like *faux foie gras*.

FAST FOOD FOR THOUGHT

According to a recent Gallup poll, 9 out of 10 elephants prefer the free peanuts that Five Guys offers its customers over the French fries and hamburgers combined.

FIVE GUYS FOIE GRAS   23

Mold the meat into a terrine of *foie gras pâté* with a nonstick mini-bread pan and serve it on a bed of lettuce — this will be the centerpiece of the platter. **Cut the toasted buns** into little bite-sized *petits toasts* and **spread the surplus of fake *pâté*** onto each. **Garnish as you wish** with the tomatoes, relish, mushrooms, and onions that we prepped earlier. *Voilà!* This *foie gras* may not exactly be derived from the fattened liver from a goose, but at least you can eat with a clearer (albeit cow-killing) conscience.

THERE'S MORE THAN ONE WAY TO KILL A GOOSE

Let's face it; slaughtering geese for *foie gras* is inhumane — and by "inhumane," I mean in*human* because really, killing geese is a lot of work for us humans. There's all that blood and feather mess to clean up, plus those geese will just *not* shut up; they freak out and honk more than cars stuck in traffic on the Santa Monica Freeway. So here are some alternative ways to kill a goose, so you can continue to turn a blind eye on the real slaughtering process:

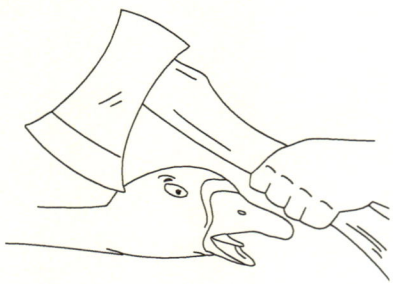

1. **Invite a goose to play "Duck Duck Goose" with other members of the poultry family.** Conveniently forget to tell them that instead of ducks, you've invited members of the NRA.

2. **Euthanasia**, the word for painless execution that scientists use on the news when they kill things and still want to look like good guys. Euthanasia is not to be confused with the homophone "youth in Asia," although I'm sure if you slipped an Asian kid a couple of new video games, he'd go kill a goose for you.

3. **Fly right into a flock of them with a commercial jet before performing an emergency landing in the Hudson River.** (Note: You may subsequently end up as an honored guest at the Super Bowl.)

4. **Tell the goose that Mother Goose wasn't its real mother and that it was adopted.** This shocking news will eventually bring it on a psychological downward spiral and a deep depression, which will ultimately lead to a heroin overdose.

AMERICAN DOMPLINGS

✱ ✱ ✱ ✱ ✱

Guaranteed in 30 minutes — but most likely more because preparation for this recipe is tedious as shit.

According to Wikipedia — the most trusted source of user-generated information on the Internet (because I just updated it to say so) — every country has its own version of dumplings. The Italians have their *ravioli*, the Polish have *pierogis*, the Japanese have *gyoza*, the Russians their *pelmeni*. However, no matter what the Internet says, when I think of the word "dumpling," what first comes to mind are the Chinese varieties, from wontons to *dim sum*.

There isn't much to be said about a classic savory dumpling in American cuisine, except for "chicken-n-dumplins," which sounds like something somebody totally made up and posted on Wikipedia. But there *should* be a Great American Dumpling in this grand land of ours, one for the culinary history books — and so we're going to make some in the most American way possible: by means of a Domino's Pizza delivered in thirty minutes. So get ready to order ahead; we're about to avoid the Noid...

Ingredients (from Domino's Pizza)

1 custom order X-Large Brooklyn-Style Pizza with light cheese, no sauce, extra Italian sausage, extra premium chicken, black olives, green peppers, mushrooms, onions, and spinach *(Note: specifically request that the pizza not be cut into slices.)*
1 bottle of water

By its basic definition, a dumpling is a morsel of dough, filled with sweet or savory ingredients. A pizza is not that different as it too includes dough topped with ingredients; we merely have to reshape the pizza into smaller dumplings.

FAST FOOD FOR THOUGHT

Why do we pronounce it "pizza" when there's no T? Hmm...

---

26 FANCY APPETIZERS

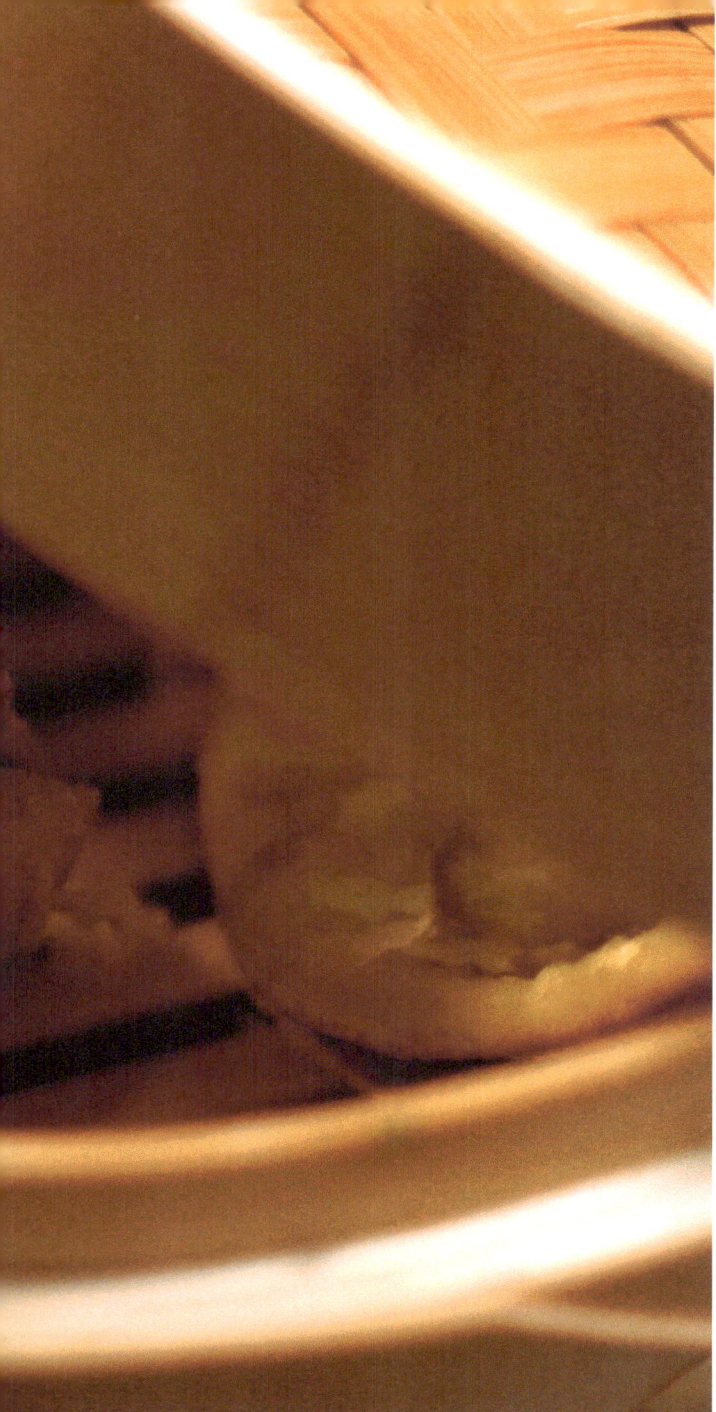

If you nicely requested that the pizza you ordered not be sliced, you'll have a nice clean slab of dough to play with. (If not, you're screwed.) Use a 5-inch circular cookie-cutter (or anything cylindrical) to **cut out as many circles out of the crust with a knife**. You should be able to cut out at least seven little circles — they will be the skins of the dumplings. **Flatten each** as much as you can with a rolling pin.

Hold one of your pizza dumpling skins in your hand and **scoop in a heaping teaspoon** of the filling. **Fold the skin in half** and then **pinch the sides inward** to form a wonton dumpling shape. If you're lucky, the cheese will work as a binding agent; if not, **use a toothpick** to keep the dumpling from falling apart. **Repeat this process over and over and over** with the rest of the dumpling skins and *presto!* You've just made the Great American Dumpling: the "Dompling." Now go alert the Interwebs!

First, **pick off all the toppings** and stick them in a food processor. **Chop them** until you have a blended paste of all the meats and vegetables; put it aside until we're ready to stuff the dough.

--- FAST FOOD FOR THOUGHT ---

The Noid, Domino's crazy claymated mascot of the '80s, spent his entire career in advertising trying to besmirch Domino's Pizza — not only on television but in video games — which probably explains why he got fired.

AMERICAN DOMPLINGS

TAPAS DE CASTILLO BLANCO

✻ ✻ ✻ ✻ ✻

High, welcome to White Castle.

Fast food chain White Castle has been a hamburger slider institution since the days of Cheech and Chong, but it was only in 2004, when it licensed its name to the film *Harold & Kumar Go To White Castle,* that it become known to the masses as the home of the only true panacea for stoners with the munchies — particularly for two Asian American dudes living in New Jersey. But you don't need to be in a marijuana-induced state of euphoria to enjoy a White Castle slider, nor do you need to be living in the state that brought us Bon Jovi, Tony Soprano, and the dance-floor phenomenon of fist-pumping. After all, anyone from anywhere can embrace their little sliders — may they come from the drive-thru window or your grocer's freezer. They are the perfect pick-me-up after a night of boozing or a date with a bong. With that said, grab yourself a Crave Case so you can make this Spanish-influenced recipe for the inner pothead in all of us.

Ingredients (from White Castle):

4 Bacon Cheeseburger Sliders
2 Chicken Sandwiches
1 order of Fried Clams
1 order of French Fries
1 order of Onion Rings
1 medium Coca-Cola (with ice)
1 medium Hi-C Poppin' Pink Lemonade (with ice)
packets of tartar sauce and ketchup

PLUS: some herbs, and not just for garnish if you know what I'm sayin' ;-)

28 FANCY APPETIZERS

First, **separate the ice from the soft drinks with a strainer** and let it melt to water; we'll use the water later. Then **pour the pink lemonade** into three wine glasses and **add enough Coke** in each glass to darken the color until it looks like a nice *rosé* wine. Then bring the remaining Coke to a boil in a nonstick saucepan and start reducing it down to a dark syrup that we will pass off as balsamic vinegar.

Next, **deconstruct everything** and **separate them into individual plates**: French fries, onion rings, fried clams, beef patties, buns, cheese, bacon, and chicken. Using a paper towel, **squeeze and dab each bun dry** of its oil and ketchup. Then place all the buns on a baking sheet and **bake them** for 10 minutes in a preheated oven at 400° F.

Meanwhile, use a food processor to **grind all the beef**, and then **hand roll it** into meatballs. **Sear the meatballs** in a pan until they start to brown. Rinse out the food processor and then **blend the French fries** into a mashed potato pulp with a little water. **Hand roll the potato pulp** into six balls.

If you got really high before trying to prepare this recipe, most likely you didn't make it past the first paragraph. You probably saw how long and instructive it was and thought, *Whoa, that's a lot of stuff,* and just sort of stared at it until the letters started looking funny. Isn't it weird when that happens? Then you probably started spacing out, staring at your kitchen wall, contemplating just eating all that food just the way it is because you've got the munchies bad, but then you took a bun off a slider and noticed that White Castle beef patties have holes in them. And you were like, *Dude, there's like, holes in my burger.* And then you wondered, *Whoa, there are five holes in my burger, and they are in the pattern of the number five like on the sides of dice.* And you continued to contemplate in your stoned state of mind, *Dude, wouldn't it be cool if there was a die with fives on all sides, so when you rolled a pair of dice you always came up with ten? Whoa, I bet that could come in pretty handy at the craps table in Vegas. I could win on hard ten bets all the time and get filthy rich and quit my job! Yeah! I would just lie on the beach and get high all day...* These thoughts continued until you got paranoid, realizing you might have left the oven on.

Holy burgers, Batman!

TAPAS DE CASTILLO BLANCO

30 Fancy Appetizers

Next, **strip off the breading from the fried clams, steam them** for a few minutes in a steamer, then **wrap one strip of bacon around a bundle of three clam strips**. Do this two more times. **Strip the breading off the chicken**, then **cut the two breasts into four halves. Finely chop** one half into smaller pieces and save the other three as is.

By now the bread in the oven should be dried out and crusty on both sides. **Grate the buns** with a grater to make a bowl of fine bread crumbs. **Crush any big chunks** into a powder as well.

In three of the potato balls, **stuff the middles with the chopped chicken**; in the other three, **stuff them with cheese**. Once they are stuffed, **roll them in the bowl of bread crumbs** until they have a generous coating. **Melt the remaining cheese** in the microwave, and use it to top the three cheese *croquetas*.

Mix four packets of tartar sauce with four packets of ketchup to make some makeshift Thousand Island dressing. You will use it as you **start to assemble each of the tapas dishes**: *anillos de cebollas* (onion rings) draped with a dollop of the dressing; the *croquetas de queso* (cheese croquettes); the *almejas* (clams) wrapped in *tocino* (bacon); the *papas rellenas de pollo* (potatoes stuffed with chicken); the *albondigas* (meatballs) served on a drizzle of the "balsamic" Coke-reduction; the remaining *tocino* garnished with herbs; and the remaining *pollo*, also garnished with herbs and some fake balsamic. **Add toothpicks to the dishes**, and then serve them with the glasses of the *"rosé."*

It sure looks fancy in the end, but if you have the munchies bad, you might as well save yourself the trouble and just eat the White Castle food as you bought it. No matter how it looks, either way, you're going to have gas in the morning.

> FAST FOOD FOR THOUGHT
>
> *This recipe has been legalized in sixteen states, but only for medicinal purposes.*

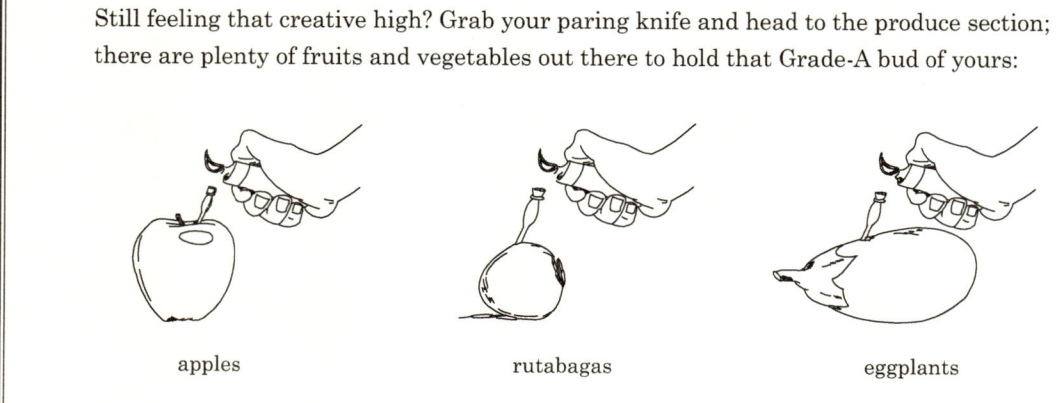

Still feeling that creative high? Grab your paring knife and head to the produce section; there are plenty of fruits and vegetables out there to hold that Grade-A bud of yours:

apples   rutabagas   eggplants

TAPAS DE CASTILLO BLANCO

Chicken soup for the soul is only good for what ails ya if you're not a soulless Wall St. executive.

FANCY SOUPS & STEWS

✳ ✳ ✳ ✳ ✳

If you don't know the classic fable "Stone Soup," it's about a mysterious traveler who enters a village and tells the villagers that he has a magic stone. This stone has the power to make the most delicious soup ever made if it's put in a cauldron of boiling water. The villagers don't believe him, so he tries to prove them wrong — but also tells them that the stone soup would be extra delicious if only he had some cabbage. So a villager contributes some cabbage and adds it to the pot. The traveler then tells them that the stone soup would be even better if only it had some carrots in it too, and so another villager contributes some carrots. The cunning traveler mentions more ingredients, which spawns more contributions, and in the end, the stupid villagers are duped into thinking the soup's delicious flavor actually comes from the stone, not their ingredients.

The moral of the story isn't about cooperation, it's that *people are dumb*; they'll eat anything you put in a pot of hot water and label "soup." Let's fill a pot with fast food and see what happens.

GAZSCHLOTZCHO

✽ ✽ ✽ ✽ ✽

Gesundheit.

Spain is amongst one of the craziest countries in the world, and I mean that in a good Spring Break sort of way, not in a supernaturally psychotic All Work And No Play Makes Spain A Dull Boy kind of way. There's never a dull moment in Spain*, for it's a nation where people get drunk on sangria and have town-wide tomato food fights when they're not busy voluntarily getting chased by stampedes of running bulls — and all just for shits and giggles. But the most insane custom that the Spaniards have shown the rest of the world is the fact that they eat *gazpacho*, their signature tomato soup, *cold*. What's even more absurd is that they pronounce it *"gathlotcho"* with a *th* sound instead of a *z*. Insanity, right? And you thought that whole Inquisition thing was crazy...

Ingredients (from Schlotzsky's):

2 Fresh Veggie Sandwiches (with extra tomatoes, extra red onions, and extra cucumber slices, but no black olives, no cheese, and no dressing)
1 Tomato Basil Soup
1 medium cup of water

PLUS: organic parsley (for garnish and an extra touch of irony)

* Except between the hours of two and five in the afternoon when everyone takes a siesta.

First, **pour the tomato basil soup in a mixing bowl**; this will be the base for what will eventually become a chunkier tomato soup. So, let's add the chunks.

Take apart the sandwiches; you ordered extra cucumbers, red onions, and tomatoes for a reason. **Dice all the cucumbers, onions, and tomatoes**, add them to the bowl and stir. There, it couldn't be easier. Now cover the bowl with plastic wrap and **stick it in the refrigerator** for a while.

When the Gazschlotzcho has chilled out, **serve it in a fancy bowl** and **garnish it** with ironic parsley. And if you're feeling extra crazy, **slice the bread** from the sandwiches and serve it on the side. ¡Buen provecho!

FAST FOOD FOR THOUGHT

"Empanada" is Spanish for "hot pocket."

GAZSCHLOTZCHO 35

THE COLONEL'S CHICKEN CORN CHOWDER

✻ ✻ ✻ ✻ ✻

It's spoon-lickin' good!

Colonel Sanders' original recipe for Kentucky Fried Chicken is confidential information, a heavily guarded secret that has endured longer than Osama bin Laden's hidden location — before we discovered he was just in the affluent Pakistani suburbs watching porn for ten years. The secret KFC recipe is locked away in a vault within a secure fortress in Louisville, Kentucky, most likely protected by the Colonel's specially trained band of ninjas. KFC has even developed security measures to keep the recipe safe from competitors (and terrorists): no one party knows the entire recipe of eleven herbs and spices, just like no one person at NORAD has the complete codes to launch nuclear warheads. There are actually two companies that mass-produce the recipe's blend for distribution; one makes the first part of the formula while the other makes the rest — then the two parts come together at the restaurant and work their combined magic of deliciousness like the strength and power of epoxy.

Many people have tried to simulate the Colonel's recipe — some even claiming that they've figured out the identities of the Secret Eleven — but their hypotheses have never been confirmed by the Colonel, nor his ranking officers at the KFC. And so the real recipe remains classified and confidential. If I were to speculate on what the Secret Eleven are, I'd say hands down one of them is definitely *salt*. Whether it is iodized, table, rock, sea, or kosher, I do not know; all I know is that if there are only five taste sensations, it is most likely *salt* in the recipe that is raising my taste buds' Kidney Stone Threat Advisory Level to orange. Seriously, after manhandling a two-piece dinner of the Colonel's chicken, you could probably smear your finger around the rim of a margarita glass instead of salting it.

Let's not and say we did, and make a KFC chowder instead...

Ingredients (from KFC):

1 KFC Original Recipe Two-Piece Breast & Wing Meal (with biscuit)
1 Corn on the Cob
1 order of Potato Wedges
1 order of Coleslaw
1 bottle of water

PLUS: organic chives (for garnish and an added touch of irony)

First, **empty the bottle of water into a pot** and **bring to a boil**. Once it is boiling, **crumble in the biscuit** little by little. **Simmer it** over a medium heat so that the starch from the biscuit thickens the chowder base.

Meanwhile, prepare the other ingredients. **Chop the potato wedges** into smaller pieces. **Remove the skin and bones** from the chicken breast and wing, then **chop the meat** into small pieces. Using a knife or corn stripper, **remove the corn kernels** from the cob. **Rinse the coleslaw** in a colander.

Once all of the biscuit has dissolved into the water, **stir in all the other ingredients** and **let it simmer** over low heat for about 10–15 minutes. When it's done, serve the chowder in a bowl and **garnish it with ironic chives**. *Voilà!* The Colonel may have his secret recipe for fried chicken locked away, but he didn't have this one for soup!

OH NO YOU DI'INT, GRANDMA!

This chowder recipe was once prepared for the Showtime cable series *Penn & Teller: Bullshit!* on an episode about fast food. It was one of three dishes prepared in an eating behavior experiment at Cornell University's Food and Brand Lab with Dr. Brian Wansink (author of *Mindless Eating*), where focus groups were brought in to sample recipes for a new bistro — but little did they know, we secretly replaced fresh ingredients with retooled fast food!

However, many people couldn't tell the difference. In fact, one man raved, "It's like something my grandma would make" — which makes you wonder, is it possible his grandmother knows the Secret Eleven herbs and spices? I don't want to be an alarmist or anything, but somebody at KFC Security better put that old grannie on a watch list.

OH, ME SO CORNY

We may be carbon-based life forms, but did you know that the body mass of most Americans is derived from corn? Think about it; corn is everywhere, and not just on the cob or in the feeds that our animals eat that ultimately end up in the meat we consume. Since the 1950s, mad scientists have been able to transform our beloved earred crops into many derivatives that appear in most of our processed foods: high fructose corn syrup, corn starch, and those weird ingredients on packages that you've always wondered about like dextrose, dextrin, maltodextrin, glucose, fructose, and their rhyming, conjoined cousin, glucose-fructose. Because of these concoctions, corn has been ubiquitous in the American diet for the past few decades; in its many shapes and forms, corn derivatives are found in many consumables: hamburgers, breakfast cereals, cough syrup, yogurt, pickles, granola bars, ketchup, ice cream, salad dressings, soda, canned soups, etc. The list goes on and on. And it's all in you.

If it's true that "you are what you eat," then most of us are made of corn. With that said, here's an artist's rendition of some of the corny people in your neighborhood.

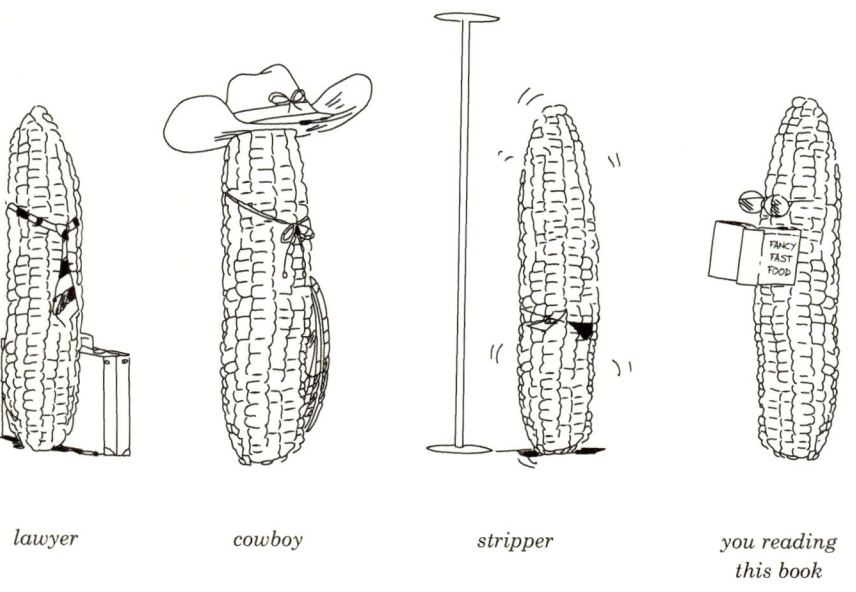

lawyer *cowboy* *stripper* *you reading this book*

FUDDJOADA

✻ ✻ ✻ ✻ ✻

What to make when you can't find that wascawy wabbit.

Feijoada, a Portuguese-Brazilian dish that dates back to the era of slavery, is a hearty meat and bean stew that became a staple meal amongst the slaves and peasants of Brazil. It was easy to make and used cheap ingredients that combined culinary thought from the African continent and the Iberian Peninsula. However, once the upper class got wind of its gastronomic appeal, it eventually became a hit amongst all classes, earning it the honor of being "Brazil's national dish." This of course is the culinary equivalent of Elvis Presley, whose handsome white boy face introduced African American-influenced rock 'n roll music to the masses in the 1950s, earning him the moniker "The King."

Traditional Brazilian feijoada uses black turtle beans, but since we are sourcing our cheap ingredients from fast food — in this case Fuddruckers — we'll just use what they've got: barbecue baked beans. Say what you will about that for now, but one day, if this recipe ever goes mainstream, it too may be given some sort of regal designation — hopefully before it gets fat and old — only to appear at Las Vegas dinner shows. *Thankyouverrrmuch.*

Ingredients (from Fuddruckers):

1 1/2 lb. Fudds Prime Hamburger (with bacon, onions, lettuce, and tomato)
1 order of Onion Rings
3 orders of BBQ Baked Beans
1 cup of water
1 condiment cup of pico de gallo
1 condiment cup of jalapeño slices
1 condiment cup of diced onions

PLUS: organic parsley (for that extra touch of elitism)

First, **peel all the breading off the onion rings**, then **dice them** and **sauté them** in a saucepan. **Add in the grilled onions** from the burger and the diced onions that you got from the fixings bar.

Dice the tomato slices from the hamburger and add them in, along with the pre-diced tomatoes of the pico de gallo. **Chop the beef patty and bacon** into smaller pieces and add those to the saucepan as well. For an extra kick, **dice the jalapeño slices** and add them too.

There's only one needed ingredient left (the one we have plenty of), so **add in all the beans**. Then **pour in a little water, stir**, and let all the flavors fuse together as it simmers over a medium heat for 10 minutes. When the bean stew is ready, simply **garnish with ironic parsley** and serve! *Bom apetite!*

BEANS, BEANS, THE MUSICAL FRUIT

You know the old children's song:

> *Beans, beans, the musical fruit —*
> *The more you eat them, the more you you toot.*
> *The more you toot, the better you feel,*
> *So let's have beans at every meal!*

Kids not only love this song because it rhymes, but because it is about one of their all-time favorite things to snicker about: farting. If you're a kid (or an immature adult) who is reading this, chances are you are snickering right now. *Plllrrrt!*

But let's be serious about this. When analyzing this finely crafted stanza of poetry, it should be noted that the children's rhyme actually *endorses* the passing of wind; farting prevents and relieves gas-induced cramps in the digestive tract — sometimes in silent but deadly ways.

However, with great flatulence comes great responsibility. Kids should learn farting etiquette at the dinner table, may it be bean-induced or otherwise. For one, be discreet when cutting the cheese; if you can't prevent yourself from floating that air biscuit, say, "Excuse me." Also, do not try to set one on fire.

If children can start behaving amidst talk of flatulence, they can grow up to be good-mannered adults and move on to snickering about other songs involving expulsions from the butt: *When you're sliding into first and you feel something burst, diarrhea, diarrhea...*

WHATAGATAWNY

✳ ✳ ✳ ✳ ✳

What happens in Texas, stays in Texas — unless it gets outsourced to India.

Mulligatawny, which sounds like an obscure compound word involving an extra stroke in golf and an old port wine, is actually derived from two Tamil words meaning "pepper water." The spicy and savory soup, which originated in India and was subsequently adopted by the British empire, has many variations — many involving ingredients *other* than pepper. There are recipes that call for apples, some that contain lentils, plus that variation that Kramer loved so much in the "Soup Nazi" episode of *Seinfeld*.

What exactly went into the recipe of the famed soup artisan was never mentioned in that episode, but I'm sure the New York-centric sitcom didn't think the character would get his ingredients from a Texas-based fast food chain. In fact, I'm sure no recipe variation of mulligatawny out there has ever dared to use items entirely from a Texan burger joint. Perhaps this is because of one particular Texas slogan printed on souvenirs found in every Texas road stop — "Don't mess with Texas" — but let's be bold, ignore that brass, and dare to do so, if only within the convenience of a kitchen.

Ingredients (from Whataburger):

2 Whatachick'ns (with extra onions)
2 Hot Apple Pies
3 whole Jalapeño Peppers
1 Vanilla Shake
1 large cup of fountain water

We are going to take the translation of "pepper water" quite literally and start with peppers. **Slice and dice the jalapeños** and put them in a big saucepan. Then, take the giant Texas-sized cup of water and **pour it all in**. **Bring the peppers and water to a boil** over a high heat.

There are so many variations of mulligatawny that it seems we can put anything in the "pepper water" and call it a day, but we're going to first add chicken. **Skin the breading off the Whatachick'n fillets** and **chop them into smaller pieces**. While you're at the cutting board, **dice the onions and some of the darker leaves of lettuce** from the sandwiches. Put all of it into the pot. To bring in a little sweetness to our spicy soup, we'll add apples from the apple pies. **Slice open one of the faces** of the crust and **scoop out the insides** into the pot.

Stir the soup as you **simmer it over a low heat** until all the flavors and colors are fused together. If you want to add a little more sweetness to take the edge off the spiciness of the "pepper water," **spoon in a dollop of milkshake**. And there you have a soup hearty enough for a Dallas cowboy — and without a huge Texas mess after all. Soup for y'all!

BIGGER THAN A DOUBLE D CUP

Soda is yet another scapegoat in the war against obesity, but let's not be so harsh; they're *soft* drinks after all, and they can provide plenty of enjoyment when you mix them with Mentos. (Look it up on YouTube if you don't know what I'm talking about.) Sure, soda has no nutritional value whatsoever, but the real root of the problem has a lot to do with today's enormous serving sizes. Large cups are getting larger, Big Gulps are getting bigger, and Super-Sizes are more super than the Man of Steel. But are we getting thirstier? Do car manufacturers really need to enable us by widening their cup holders? Is it really necessary to disguise a whole liter bottle of soda by putting it in a paper cup with a straw on top?

I'm all for bringing the fast food beverage sizes back to the way they were before inflation, a time when the current "kid's" size was the "small," the "small" was the "medium," the "medium" was the "large," and the "large" was used for popcorn. If that ever happened, we'd have a whole lot of really big paper cups to get rid of — but rather than throw them right into the recycle bin, we could repurpose them for other uses:

- paint it black, loop a belt around it, and tape a ring of black construction paper to the rim so that your kid can use it when he plays Myles Standish in the local elementary school's Thanksgiving play

- paint it orange, tape on a rubber base, and use it as a traffic cone

- set up a beer pong tournament for those giant tree people in *Lord of the Rings*

- fasten a strap on it and use it to hold pounds of candy when you go trick-or-treating

- use it to finally transfer that fern into a bigger pot before you kill yet another houseplant

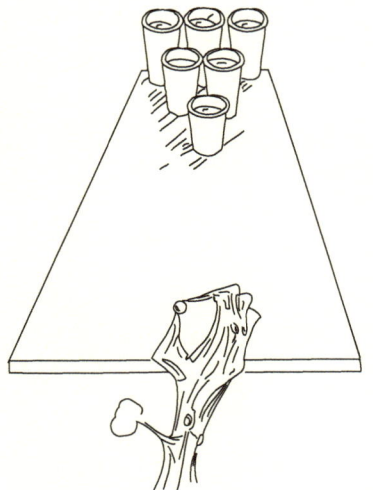

MOE'S SOUTHWEST CASSOULET

✳ ✳ ✳ ✳ ✳

Bienvenue à Chez Moe!

"Moe" may be a name associated with the southwest of America for Tex-Mex fast food, but there exists another Moe — in another southwestern region — at least for the sake of this recipe's preamble. Moe (which is short for "Maurice," of course) resides in Castelnaudary, France, the self-proclaimed *"Capitale du Cassoulet"* in the southern Languedoc-Roussillon region, where he is actually inspired by Tex-Mex fast food for his variation of the traditional French dish (if you can suspend disbelief). Here's his recipe:

Ingredients (from Moe's Southwest Grill):

2 Pulled Pork Tacos (hard shells with extra pork and no cheese) with a side of beans
1 Salad with double pulled pork
1 extra bowl of Beans
2 condiment cups of Kaiser Salsa
1 cup of water

PLUS: organic parsley (for garnish and a touch of irony)

SOME OTHER MOES

Food(ography)'s Mo Rocca

Moe Howard from The Three Stooges

Moe Murdock, the guy who drew these

PICTURE NOT AVAILABLE

Mo', the Prophet Mohammed

First, **extract all the pulled pork** from the tacos and the salad. **Do the same with the beans** and put them in a big mixing bowl; **add the extra beans** as well. What's left is the salad; **chop some of it** and **add it to another prep bowl** with the salsa.

Pour all the beans in a saucepan over a medium heat and pour in a little water. As this is stewing, **add in the salsa mixture and half of the pulled pork** — save the other half for when we plate our creation. Cover the saucepan and let it **simmer over a low heat** for about 10 minutes. Meanwhile, take the hard taco shells and **grind them in a food processor** until they become crumbs, which will be used for a garnish.

When it's ready, simply **serve the cassoulet** in a bowl, **pile some pork on top,** and **sprinkle the top with taco shell crumbs**. Garnish with ironic parsley and serve! *Está magnifique!*

Soniccian Borscht

❊ ❊ ❊ ❊ ❊

это предложение в русском

Unbeknownst to most of the world is the tiny Eastern European nation of Soniccia, a country whose traditions have carried on through the ages, even before the bleak days of the Soviet Union. So small that it is barely mentioned as a former Soviet republic, Soniccia strives to sustain a unique national identity in the post-Cold War era, much like some of its sibling nations: Latvia, Ukraine, and Georgia. This distinction of national identity is most evident in Soniccian cuisine; while other former Soviet republics' variations of the age-old, beet-based soup of *borscht* remain in the savory category, Soniccia's palate is bit more on the sweet side.

Obtaining ingredients for this recipe in Soniccia isn't quite as easy as it is in most parts of the modern Western World. Soniccian culture still hasn't evolved from some of its former Soviet routines; one cannot simply buy fast food goods off the shelf or order them from a person behind a counter. Instead, you must order the items the old-fashioned way, by pushing a button on an antiquated intercom system while remaining inside your vehicle. (This is after having had to wait in a long queue of other vehicles already, at certain times during the day.) This ordering process is so prevalent in Soniccia that even if you wish to go on foot and walk to the food establishment to buy goods, you must still push a button and order from the intercom system. Only when your order is confirmed over the speaker does a person bring you your items — sometimes (but not always) using vintage roller skates from before the Iron Curtain went up.

In case you hadn't figured it out already, this country is completely made up. The former Soviet republic of "Soniccia" doesn't actually exist; it was just a joke about Sonic's old-fashioned intercom-only ordering process. So buck up, comrades, the Cold War is still over — even if this mock soup recipe is made from *frosty dessert treats*.

Ingredients (from Sonic):

2 large Cherry Limeade Chillers
2 orders of Apple Slices
1 Fresh Banana (from the Everyday Value Menu)
1 Vanilla Dish (ice cream)

First, **strain the two cherry limeades** to extract and pour the red liquid into two separate pieces of cookware: a saucepan and a nonstick skillet. **Save the wedges of lime** as you will use them for garnish later. **Bring both the saucepan and skillet to a boil** with high heat. While waiting for them to start bubbling, you can prepare the other items.

Slice the apple wedges into thin ribbons with a sharp knife, following the curve of each apple wedge's shape when it's laying flat on a cutting board. (This will make them resemble shreds of cabbage.) Once you have a favorable amount of apple shreds, **add them to the boiling saucepan of cherry limeade**. Reduce it to a low heat and **let it simmer**, allowing the apples to absorb the dark red color.

The contents of the skillet should be boiling by now too, but **let it continue to boil**, uncovered. The limeade will eventually be reduced down to a thick, red syrup. In the meantime, **slice the banana** into smaller chunks. When the red syrup is ready, **infuse the banana** with it so that the chunks resemble beets.

For a contrasting green garnish, **slice the rinds off the lime wedges** and then **chop them** into smaller pieces.

Finally, assemble your sweet Soniccian delicacy: **ladle out the apple-stewed soup** into a fancy bowl and then **add some beet-looking banana chunks**. Instead of serving it with sour cream as they do in Russia and Poland, **add a dollop of vanilla ice cream** and then **garnish the top with the chopped lime zest**. And there it is! Perfect for a hot summer day, whether you are in the fictitious nation of Soniccia or not!

--- TIPS FROM AN EMPTY JAR ---

Sonic's carhops aren't giving you a hint that you have bad breath when they give you that after-meal mint — they've been doing that since the 1950s — unless of course you're eating something with raw onions, in which case they probably are.

DRIVE-THRU ETIQUETTE

Who says table manners have to be confined to the table at a fancy restaurant? You should still be polite and well-behaved whenever you're dining at any establishment, even if you're just in your car and the waiter is some pimply teen who wouldn't know which white wine to pair with that Filet-O-Fish. Here are some tips on drive-thru etiquette, so you can mind your *p*'s and *q*'s without even leaving your vehicle:

1. **Know before you go.** Have a good idea of what you want ahead of time so that you don't hold up the line too much. Remember, there's no need to wait and hear what the daily specials are, or what the soup of the day is, because there aren't any. If you're being indecisive, just close your eyes and say, "Number One with a Coke" — it's a phrase that's guaranteed to get you something decent in almost every scenario. (A "Number Two with a Coke" on the other hand, could get you some really nasty and unsanitary results.)

2. **Speak clearly when you order.** In many cases, the intercom system will be spotty and the person taking your order will sound like she's talking on an iPhone with crappy cell reception. Speak slowly and clearly, and repeat your order as necessary so there's no confusion if they hear "trip her wit' ease" when you're trying to order that Triple Whopper with Cheese.

3. **Check your bag and keep your cool.** If they messed up your order, save face and nicely point out the mistakes so they can adjust it promptly. There's no need to get upset at the employee manning the window; he's probably already full of angst as it is. If you really want to get back at him and have the time to do so, just annoy him with repeated requests for extra ketchup packets and extra salt and pepper. Then ask for extra napkins and extra straws. Then, when he thinks he's done with you, ask for one more packet of ketchup. (You'd be annoyed too, huh?)

4. **Don't honk if you're impatient.** Honking your horn won't speed anything up; it will only aggravate the people ahead of you — road rage belongs on the road, not at the drive-thru. If you're that impatient to get your food, pull into a parking space and walk your lazy ass inside; there's usually less of a wait inside whenever there are six or more cars lined up outside. And let's face it; you could probably use the exercise anyway.

Chicken McNuggets sure do look big when you zoom up really close.

FANCY POULTRY

✻ ✻ ✻ ✻ ✻

You know the age-old question: Which came first, the chicken or the egg? Well, in fast food terms, obviously the answer is the *egg* — but only until 11 a.m. when they stop serving breakfast and switch over to the eggless lunch/dinner menu. Then again, some fast food places now serve chicken biscuits in the morning, so that metaphorical early birds can catch — and get their fix on — early birds.

The food industry knows we can't get enough of chicken; it's a staple in the public's diet, may it be fried, fricasseéd, or processed into nuggets in the shapes of dinosaurs. Chicken is versatile like that; its breasts, wings, legs, and thighs can be braised or barbecued, spiced or sesame'd, shredded or breaded, sandwiched or skewered, baked or buffalo'd — or put under the culinary command of General Tso. You can eat chicken in a box, or you can eat it with a fox — the possibilities are limitless! So go ahead and count your chickens before they hatch; there's plenty more where that came from, waiting to cross over from the other side of the proverbial road.

CHICKEN, CHEDDAR & MUSHROOM ZOUFFLÉ

✽ ✽ ✽ ✽ ✽

Turn it up to eleven.

If there's anything that I've learned from old classic cartoons, it's the Hierarchy of Domesticated Animals: dogs chase cats, cats chase mice, and mice chase hunks of cheese. The other thing I've learned is that when you're making a soufflé, you have to be really wary of loud noises so that the cartoon depiction of said soufflé doesn't deflate with the sound effect of a whoopee cushion. *Pfffllllleeeeeeurrt...*

In reality, soufflés aren't that unstable, nor are they terribly difficult to prepare — especially when you're not using any raw eggs and just faking it with fast food items. So go ahead and be as loud as you want — bang on your pots and pans even —because this soufflé will "rise" even without that funny, uplifting cartoon sound effect of a slide whistle. *Whoooooohhhwp!*

**Ingredients
(from Zaxby's):**

1 Chicken Finger Plate
  (with Texas Toast)
2 extra orders of Texas Toast
1 order of Fried White Cheddar Bites
1 order of Fried Mushrooms
1 Side Salad
1 cup of water

PLUS: organic chives (for garnish and an added touch of irony)

54 FANCY POULTRY

First, **skin the chicken fingers** so you are left with only the breast meat, and then **cut it into small cubes. Rinse all of it in a colander** to get rid of any residual breading.

Next, use your fingers to **peel off the breading from the fried mushrooms. Rinse them** to get rid of any residual breading as well. Use a paring knife to **cut the breading off the white cheddar bites**, then **grate the cheese chunks** found inside. Also, **chop some lettuce** from the side salad.

Put the mushrooms, cheese, and lettuce in a food processor and then **add in pieces of the Texas toast**. Add some water and then **blend** — it will eventually turn into a dough.

Put the dough in a big mixing bowl and then **incorporate the cubed chicken. Mix well** until the chicken is evenly distributed.

Using a rubber spatula, **transfer the mixture into a ramekin**. The dough should be dense enough to mold and sculpt, so **use the rubber spatula to shape up the top above the rim**, so it gives the illusion that the soufflé has risen by itself. Put the ramekin in a preheated oven at 400°F and **bake for 15 minutes** until the top develops a crust.

When it's done, let it cool and then **garnish it with ironic chives** for that extra splash of color to break the soufflé's monotone. Now serve it as loud as you want!

INGREDIENTS AND INNUENDO

No matter how you rearrange it, chicken entrées will still taste like chicken — even if its plating may imply something else:

Baked chicken breast topped with portabello mushrooms and roasted red peppers looks more a lot like a "clam" than poultry.

Be careful when slicing this chicken roulade with spinach and cheese; the creamy inside may start to ooze out. (How's that for "food porn?")

Two chicken legs with sriracha sauce and green onions may look like a yin-yang, but to others, it's a 14-year-old boy's favorite number.

LE CHICKEN McCONFIT

✻ ✻ ✻ ✻ ✻

It's McNifique!

There's an ancient preservation technique in which animal flesh is first fused with sodium chloride and then boiled in a solution of adipose tissue that has been melted into a liquid state. Interesting, eh? Leave it to the French for taking what sounds like a mummification experiment and calling it something that sounds appetizing: *confit* (pronounced *kohn-fee*). Then again, you can't always make cooking sound appetizing in English when you break it down into science — unless you're Alton Brown.

In gourmet terms, a confit is when poultry (and sometimes pork) is preserved — or simply served — after salting it and slow-cooking it in its own fat. When you define it that way, it sounds truly delectable to any discerning epicure, as long as she doesn't mind putting on a couple of pounds. The scientific irony is, the animal fat that is eaten eventually gets converted into human fat — which makes you wonder what percentage of chicken or pork fat make up the contents inside the vats outside of a liposuction clinic.

Anyway, forget about science; this is a satirical cookbook after all. Let's take some greasy McDonald's food in lieu of natural ingredients, so that we can be gourmets and take the French's affection for fat to another level — down, that is.

Ingredients (from McDonald's):

1 10-Piece Chicken McNuggets
1 large order of French Fries
1 Fruit & Walnut Salad
packets of Barbecue, Sweet 'n Sour, and Hot Mustard Sauces
2 bottles of water

PLUS: organic chives (for garnish and an extra touch of irony)

For this recipe, we will consider the fattiest part of the McNugget to be its breading; after all, it soaks in and retains a lot of the fatty frying oils. **Skin the McNuggets** with a paring knife until you have a pile of McNugget skins. **Put these McSkins in a food processor** with about half a bottle of water and purée it until it looks like fatty goop.

Pour the McMush into a nonstick skillet, add some more water, and **bring it to a boil**. Once it is bubbling, simmer it down and **place the McNugget meat in the skillet**. Cover and let it stew over a low heat for about half an hour.

Meanwhile, clean out your food processor and then **blend down the fries**, adding water as needed, until it all becomes a soft potato purée. Next, take some apple slices from the fruit and walnut salad and **slice them into thinner slivers** with a knife. Finally, **mix the dipping sauces** of your preference in a cup and stir until it has a consistent color.

TIPS FROM AN EMPTY JAR

If you find a chicken head in your box of McNuggets, don't be so quick to sue McDonald's; you can give it a fancy name and pass it off as an exotic and bizarre food. Alternatively, you give it a silly name and use it in a finger puppet show.

After the McMorsels of fat-stewed chicken have cooled down, plate the dish: **put the potato purée in the center of a fancy white plate**, then **top it with a layer of apple slices**. **Butterfly cut your McNuggets-turned-McConfit pieces** and then **place them on top of the apple slices**. **Drizzle the sauce** around the plate and then **garnish with some chopped walnuts**. **Top it off with some slices of organic chives** and serve your soft drink in a wine glass. *Voilà!* Did somebody say McConfit?

KNOW YOUR McNUGGETS

All fast food connoisseurs should know their Chicken McNuggets. While the four, six, ten, or twenty pieces all contain the battered, deep-fried goodness of "all white meat chicken," they come in just three basic shapes, each of which has its own unique characteristics:

This oval-shaped McNugget is not completely round for good reason; one end is narrower, acting as the perfect handle to daintily dip it in Barbecue Sauce with your pinky finger pointed outwards.

Celebrities that look like this shape include: **Tyra Banks**

This elegant McNugget of straight lines and rounded corners seems to say, "I am a work of art, but please feel free to dip me in Sweet 'n Sour Sauce and eat me."

Celebrity that looks like this shape (and could use a little dip in Sweet 'n Sour Sauce): **Brad Pitt**

Squint your eyes and this McNugget resembles a Christmas stocking. This of course means that it can be Christmas year round (in your mouth) and is best served with the Egg Nog shake in the winter.

Uncanny celebrity look-alike: **Jay Leno**

LE CHICKEN McCONFIT

JACK IN THE BENTO

✺ ✺ ✺ ✺ ✺

Pop goes the katsu.

Over the decades, the creations of the Japanese have made their way into many aspects of our world: electronics, automobiles, video games, Mr. Miyagi, green tea Frappuccinos, sushi, and plastic food meticulously made to look like sushi, to name a few. The Japanese have also entertained us with their *Seven Samurai*, the *Godzilla* movies, anime cartoons, and those wacky game shows where contestants run around crazy obstacle courses before inevitably falling in water, only to be ridiculed by Japanese commentators who are poorly dubbed in English. Another Japanese creation is *Iron Chef* — the original food challenge show — in which chefs duked it out by preparing dishes from a secret ingredient in order to impress a panel of food critics — including one recurring female actress who always giggled like a Japanese schoolgirl. (Japan also gave us giggling Japanese schoolgirls.)

No matter how innovative or humorous these creations may be, the Japanese still retain a distinct sense of style in everything they do, and it's evident in their food presentation. When they arrange a meal in a sectionalized tray, it's stylish and elegant, and often comes as a pretty good lunch special with a miso soup: the *bento*, the Japanese word for "box." This contrasts with a similar American invention; we microwave frozen food in a sectionalized tray and call it a "TV dinner." However, our convenience food doesn't need to look so crude; here's a way to transform that Jack in the Box takeout into a fancy Japanese "TV dinner" to eat while you sit in front of the boob tube watching those wacky Japanese-import game shows, waiting for the next contestant to fall down.

Ingredients (from Jack in the Box):

1 Chipotle Chicken Ciabatta with Spicy Crispy Chicken
1 Steak Teriyaki Bowl
1 Side Salad
1 large Coke

First, **pour about half of the large Coke in a nonstick skillet** and start reducing it over a medium heat — the Coke reduction will be used later. Then, disassemble your items to **sort out the ingredients** you need: ciabatta bread, steak pieces, a chicken cutlet, rice, broccoli, lettuce, carrots, cucumber, and cherry tomatoes.

Rinse the rice in a colander and then **dry it out** with some paper towels. Let it sit out and get sticky for a bit while you prepare the "nori sheets": **thinly slice pieces of the ciabatta bread** and then **dye it to a darker color** in the Coke reduction. Let the nori sheets cool so that you can handle them, but don't let them completely cool and dry out. When it's okay to touch, **place the darker side down**, and **top it with rice. Roll it** as best you can, then **cut off the ends** to even it out. **Slice some cucumber** and insert a piece in the center of the "maki" roll piece, along with a strand of carrot. Do this at least two more times for more pieces of sushi.

Dice down the steak pieces until they almost become a paste. Then **place the steak in the skillet** with the remaining Coke and **bring to a boil**. This concoction should be thick like a katsu curry sauce, so **add torn pieces of bread** as needed so that it dissolves and gives the sauce some density. **Stir it** until everything becomes consistent.

The main entrée, the chicken katsu, is the easiest part to prep; simply **cut the spicy chicken cutlet** into pieces about ¾-inch wide. Finally, the assembly: in a bento box, **place the rice** in one section, pat it down, and **garnish it with a cherry tomato** in the center. **Place the makeshift maki rolls** in the corner section, and the **lettuce and the remaining carrots** in the salad section. For the main area, **pour a layer of the "curry" sauce**, then **place the chicken katsu on top** with a garnish of broccoli. For an extra touch, take some squishy broccoli and **mush it with your fingers** into a ball so that it looks like a wad of wasabi paste. *Hai!*

FAST FOOD FOR THOUGHT

If you counted the amount of apples bitten into at the beginning of every episode of every version of Iron Chef, you'd have enough apples to make one big-ass pie, 37 feet wide in diameter.

COQ AU CHEERVIN

✸ ✸ ✸ ✸ ✸

Cheer up with a little southern hospitality.

If you're a hungry carnivore spending any amount of time in the Carolinas, you will undoubtedly be stuffing your face with signature dishes like Carolina pulled pork or deliciously greasy fried chicken. And while you may enjoy it with an ice-cold Carolina Pale Ale, a sweet tea, or a growler of moonshine, the most cheerful way to wash it all down is with a nice glass of Carolina-based Cheerwine. For all you Yankees who aren't privy to this sweet concoction found in many places below the Mason Dixon Line, Cheerwine is a sweet and bubbly cherry libation unlike any other, with a deep burgundy color like a fine Pinot Noir. However there is no alcohol in it, so don't get your hopes up if you're an underage teen trying to score some booze for that weekend party while your parents are away.

Let's pretend we're in a fancy Carolina restaurant ordering fried chicken. What wine do we pair it with? Cheerwine, of course. But let's pair them even further by making a mock recipe of the French classic, *coq au vin*. Just remember to pronounce *"coq au cheervin"* with a French accent *(kohk oh sheer vaehn')* and serve the remaining Cheerwine in fancy stemware. You'll appear older and sophisticated, and if you play it cool, maybe you'll even be able to score some liquor. If not, there's got to be some bootleg moonshine *some*where in them thar hills.

Ingredients (from Bojangles'):

1 Two-Piece Fried Chicken Dinner (leg & thigh) with:
1 Biscuit
1 side of Coleslaw
1 side of Dirty Rice
1 side of Green Beans
1 large cup of Cheerwine
packets of salt, pepper, and hot sauce

First, **pour two-thirds of the Cheerwine into a saucepan** — saving the rest to serve in a wine glass during the meal — and **bring it to a boil**. In lieu of the unavailable ingredients for a proper *coq au vin* (mushrooms, onions, lardons), **spice the stew** with our packets of salt, pepper, and hot sauce.

Next, **slice the biscuit in two** and **bake it** in a preheated oven at 400° F until it becomes hard and crusty. **Let it cool** before **grinding it down into bread crumbs** with a food processor. We will use this to coat our chicken pieces as well as add a little thickness to the stew since it is entirely made of starch and fat.

Skin the two pieces of chicken and then **bread them with the bread crumbs** in a big mixing bowl. Once they are coated, drop them into the saucepan and **let them stew** for a while, until the meat absorbs all of the red cherry goodness.

Coq Au Cheervin 65

In the meantime, **rinse the coleslaw** and **add it to the dirty rice. Arrange the cut green beans** on a plate back into the form of the whole string beans they came from.

Finally, plate your fancy dish: **add the Coq Au CheerVin chicken pieces** to the rice and green beans, along with some sauce. Don't forget to **pour some of the remaining Cheerwine in a wine glass...** *Clink!*

TIPS FROM AN EMPTY JAR

If you want to be really chichi, stick your nose in the air and refer to the blended dirty rice only as "rice pilaf," and the green beans only as "haricots verts."

LET'S BOUGIE

Being sophisticated is more than gettin' your hair did, dressing up in fancy threads, and saying things with a Eurotrash accent. It's all about having an air of debonair, a dash of panache, and an extra bit of ego. Here are some ways to be that urbane jerk when doing ordinary everyday things:

- Always drink water out of a fancy wine glass with a twist of lemon, even if you're just working out at the gym or taking a break from moving furniture.

- Say elitist things like, "I read about it in *The New York Times*," even if the story you're sharing is the one you just read in *Us Weekly* about how Brangelina eats pizza just like us!

- Drive up to cars and ask the drivers if they have any Grey Poupon.

- Introduce yourself at parties with your last name, followed by your first and last name — even if you're not a secret agent greeting your arch nemesis bent on world domination.

- Eat your Snickers with a knife and fork à la George Costanza; scoff at people who eat it with their hands.

- Don't always drink beer — but when you do, make it a Dos Equis.

- Always leave yourself a chocolate mint on your pillow for the next bedtime.

- Serve your fast food all fancy! (Obviously.)

CHICKEN PIZZA MASALA

✻ ✻ ✻ ✻ ✻

It's another red dot special.

Before there were Bollywood stars and slumdog millionaires, India's elite was comprised of the ruling class of maharajas, many of which sported big mustaches (before they were considered ironically trendy by hipsters). From within their royal palaces, the maharajas could snap their royal fingers and order whatever they wanted, from sparkling royal jewels to royal elephant rides to royal samosas served on royal plates — all while performing pages 112–114 of the *Kama Sutra* with their royal concubines, if they so desired. However, the age of the maharajas ended in 1971 when Parliament was instated, scrapping the maharajas of any real power or popularity — but hey, at least their mustaches are still considered hip by some.

If I were an all-powerful maharaja in this day and age, I'd snap my fingers and have someone combine two of my favorite foods — chicken tikka masala and pizza — for a royal snack in between *Kama Sutra* positions, of course. Alas, those days are over (nor am I a maharaja), so I guess I could just combine the two foods myself. So can you:

Ingredients (from Pizza Hut):

1 medium Hand-Tossed Style Pizza with chicken, onions, and tomatoes; extra sauce, but easy on the cheese (*Note: specifically request that the pizza not be cut into slices.*)
1 order of Buffalo Wings (6) with blue cheese dressing (2)
3 orders of Marinara Sauce
1 bottle of water

PLUS: organic coriander (for garnish and a touch of mustache-sporting-hipster irony)

First, **pick the chicken, tomatoes, and onions off the pizza pie** and put them to the side. Then, using a fork, **scrape off the cheese** so that the only thing remaining is an unsliced slab of crust. Take the crust and **flatten it further with a rolling pin**. When you fold it, it sort of looks like naan, which is the perfect accompaniment for the dish we will throw together with the rest of the ingredients.

Put the chicken, tomatoes, onions, and cheese into a medium saucepan over a medium heat. **Stir in all the marinara sauce**, followed by all the **blue cheese dressing**. When it's all mixed together, it should start to resemble the orange hue of a masala sauce. **Add in the chicken wings** and **smother them** until they are well coated.

Finally, the plating: **spoon the chicken pizza masala** into a small serving dish and **garnish it** with some chopped ironic coriander. Serve it with the fake naan. Now you have a dish fit for a maharaja — whether he's in power or not — to enjoy during a break between the "Peacock" and "Milch Cow" positions.

--- FAST FOOD FOR THOUGHT ---

Cows are considered sacred in India, so the McDonald's restaurants there don't serve beef. Instead of the two-all-beef patty-laden Big Mac, they serve the non-beef "Chicken Maharaja-Mac" — which is a pretty good idea considering the stray holy cows in Delhi roam the streets rummaging through garbage all day. How's that for junk food?

CHICKEN PIZZA MASALA

CHICKEN MOLE FROSTANO

✻ ✻ ✻ ✻ ✻

"All you need is love — but a little chocolate now and then doesn't hurt."
–Lucy Van Pelt

Everyone loves chocolate — any sane person, that is. It's true; unless you're one of those fascists who hate chocolate, the world of gastronomy agrees it's a wonderful thing in its many shapes and forms. Chocolate can be served hot as fudge or frozen as ice cream, melted in fondue *caquelons* or within eponymous chip cookies, formed into little round bon-bons or in the shape of Easter bunnies, or molded in its most common form, the bar — coincidentally, the perfect medium for distributing Golden Tickets. Chocolate flows in the river of our pure, sweet-toothed imagination. It's considered better than therapy by some, and an aphrodisiac by others. Also, it makes people just *cuckoo* for Cocoa Puffs.

Some people love chocolate so much that they'll find any way to consume more of it*, particularly the Mexicans, who have ingeniously managed to get away with coming to this country and mixing it in one of their classic chicken dishes. While the word *mole* (rhymes with "obey," not "bowl") is merely Mexican Spanish for "sauce" or "concoction," it has come to be associated with the classic chocolate-based spicy sauce from the Mexican state of Puebla. If not for the Mexican chefs who have been adding chocolate to this spicy sauce for centuries, I might have not known what to do with that Chocolate Fudge Chocolate Frosty Shake from Wendy's when preparing this mock recipe — other than drink it and chase it down with a Yoo-hoo like a normal chocoholic.

---

* A chocolate-chip chocolate ice cream sundae, for example, topped with hot fudge and chocolate sprinkles, served on top of a chocolate fudge brownie — all melted, puréed, and administered intravenously if need be.

Ingredients (from Wendy's):

1 order of Spicy Chipotle Boneless Wings
1 Chocolate Fudge Frosty Shake
1 Spicy Chicken Wrap
1 side order of Chili (with crackers)
packets of Hot Chili Sauce

PLUS: organic Mexican cilantro (for garnish and a touch of Mexican irony)

Let's start with the savory and spicy element of mole sauce first. **Strain the chili over a saucepan** so that you extract all of the tomato-based sauce. **Add in the packets of hot sauce** for that extra kick. Then **spoon in some Chocolate Fudge Frosty** into the mix and stir it over a medium heat.

Next, use your fingers and/or a fork to **shred the boneless "wings"** into a pile. There's no need to rinse off the spicy chipotle sauce off; it will only add to the overall flavor of this dish. While you're at it, **skin the spicy chicken** from the wrap and shred that too — but **make sure you keep the tortilla intact**. Then **stir in all the shredded chicken** to the sauce and **let it simmer** for 15–20 minutes, so all the spicy and sweet flavors get infused with the meat.

Rinse the tortilla off and **pat it dry** with a paper towel; it will serve as the bed for your spicy chicken and chocolate stew. **Place the tortilla in the center of a fancy plate**, and then generously **spoon some of our Chicken Mole Frostano** in the center. **Crush the crackers** while they're still in their little packet so they slightly resemble sesame seeds, and **use them as a garnish** to sprinkle on top. For a splash of color, also **add some chopped cilantro** for that extra touch of irony. Serve and enjoy! ¡Olé!

FAST FOOD FOR THOUGHT

"Boneless wings" are just a marketing ploy conjured up by the fast food industry for chicken breasts that don't know how to fly.

TIPS FROM AN EMPTY JAR

Like with any unused fast food ingredient, you can always eat the unfancy, unused chili — or give it to your pet dog. (You might want to bring an extra pooper scooper bag on your next walk though.)

A GUIDE TO PICKIN' CHICKEN

If you have the time on your hands, you may find yourself preparing *real* chicken instead of the greasy fast variety used as ingredients in this parody of a cookbook. However, in today's world of food source scrutiny, picking a raw chicken has gotten a little confusing since it goes beyond the familiar choices of crispy or grilled, spicy or mild, extra crispy or original recipe. The general rule of thumb is if a packaged raw chicken is the color of Fritos, chances are it's been unnaturally processed like Fritos — which may be okay with you if you're sporting a fake orange hue after that session you spent at the tanning salon.

Here's a guide to those buzz words found on the labels in your grocer's poultry department, so you can pick the chicken that best fits your personality:

"Organic." These chickens are quite studious since they have to pass a series of tests to be certified, like public accountants. Not only are they raised naturally, but they are also very good at math.

"Free Range." These birds aren't cooped up inside, sitting on their asses while watching mindless reality TV all day; they are outdoorsy types that are free to go out for a little exercise, may it be running, trying to fly, or low-impact pilates.

"Hormone/Steroid-free." These chickens are happy just the way they are; they aren't juiced up and buff like some bodybuilding chickens, nor did they get boob jobs.

"Air-Chilled." These laid-back birds just can't stand the heat and prefer to just chillax in the comforts of air-conditioning.

"Antibiotic-free." These are chickens of the Christian Scientist faith, who don't believe in medicine, even if there's a bird flu epidemic going on.

"Kosher." These Jewish, guilt-laden fowl don't take cream in their coffee when pecking amongst themselves.

"Halal." These Allah-praising chickens lead peace-filled lives, even though that image has been marred these days by extremist cockfighting chickens.

Vegetarians need not apply.

FANCY MEATS

* * * * *

Years ago, a sage old woman, after a moment of deep contemplative thought, asked a profound question on everyone's mind: "*Where's* the beef?" The answer is, it's in you, it's in me, it's in the bellies of all us Americans, minus all the vegetarian tree-huggers out there. The average meat-eating American consumes a whopping 200 pounds of meat a year — enough meat to make a whopping Whopper patty approximately 334 feet in diameter. That would not only require a really big bun, but a really big mouth — and not the type of big mouth like your friend's, who couldn't help but ruin the surprise twist of that M. Night Shyamalan movie.

Why do we consume so much meat? Because it's *delicious*, that's why. And besides, it's always the hit of a party. What's a barbecue, Super Bowl bash, or Hawaiian vacation resort luau without meat? Meat has been interwoven into our social fabric; it's what's for dinner, it's what's for lunch, and it's here to stay. So go ahead and eat that extra hamburger — triple bypass surgery was invented for a reason.

BEEF WELLINGTON, ANIMAL STYLE

❋ ❋ ❋ ❋ ❋

Animals never did it this way on The Discovery Channel.

So they may not be listed on the menu, but the "secret" unadvertised items at In-N-Out Burger haven't exactly been confidential with foodie bloggers out there revealing them like it's some scandalous exposé. Mind you, it's not a big scandal at all; there are no bloody gloves, no wiretaps, no stained dresses — well, maybe some ketchup stains, not the other kind. In recent years, In-N-Out has come forward and embraced the rumors, confirmed they were true, and even posted them on their website's "Not-So-Secret Menu" for everyone to see.

So ordering a burger "Animal Style" may not be such a secret; it's a burger with lettuce, tomatoes, mustard, pickles, and onions, all bound together by their special but sloppy Thousand Island-esque spread. There, I revealed it. But psst... Did you know you can make a variation of Beef Wellington out of In-N-Out burgers and sides? Let's keep this secret to ourselves, shall we? If not, we'll have to hunt you down — like animals.

**Ingredients
(from In-N-Out Burger):**

3 In-N-Out Hamburgers
   (Animal Style)
1 order of French Fries
1 cup of water
salt and pepper packets

PLUS: a sprig of organic thyme
   (for garnish and an extra touch
   of irony)

First, take the buns from the burgers and **scrape off all the Animal Style toppings into a bowl** – save those for later. **Put the buns in a food processor**, add a little bit of water, and **blend it back down to a moldable dough**. Then, using a rubber spatula and rolling pin, **spread the dough flat** onto a large nonstick baking sheet. **Bake it** in a preheated oven at 400°F for 5–10 minutes. When it develops a flaky, pie-like crust, take it out and **let it cool** on the baking sheet for a bit so it's easy to lift off the pan with a spatula when you're ready.

Next, let's prep the Animal Style toppings. **Chop them all together in a food processor** until it becomes a chunky spread. Use a

— FAST FOOD FOR THOUGHT —

It's ironic that it's called "Animal Style," even though the all toppings are vegetarian, with no addition of any animal meats — not even soy substitutes.

BEEF WELLINGTON, ANIMAL STYLE

rubber spatula to **evenly spread a layer** of this Animal Style dressing over the pastry.

Cut the burger patties into smaller chunks so you can **put them in a food processor** and revert them to ground beef. Then, using your hands, **mold the beef** into a small, long slab of meat — it's to be the "beef tenderloin" of our "Beef Wellington." **Place it in the center of the baking sheet**, then carefully **fold the crust over it** from the bottom, then the top. Fold over the sides until it's completely covered with the crust. For the side dish, mash some potatoes by **blending fries in a food processor** with a little water.

Finally, the plating: **slice the crusted meatloaf** into serving portions; use two per plate. **Garnish it** with an ironic sprig of thyme. *Tada!* Beef Wellington, Animal Style! *Roar!*

OTHER THINGS YOU CAN MOLD WITH MUSHY BREAD

a bread bowl

a mug

a replica of that lopsided ashtray you made in the third grade

a sad rendition of the Venus di Milo

CARLBONADE FLAMANDE

✻ ✻ ✻ ✻ ✻

"No soldier can fight unless he is properly fed on beef and beer."
–John Churchill

When you think of Belgium, several images may (or may not) come to mind: dark Belgian chocolates, fruit-covered Belgian waffles, or scenes from the movie *Timecop*, starring Belgian action star Jean-Claude Van Damme. Thankfully the contributions of Belgium don't end with the "Muscles from Brussels"; let us not forget that the Belgians also gave us Baroque painters and old-fashioned beers. Belgian beers and ales are highly-respected around the world, particularly the Trappist ales, brewed by a special order of pious Catholic monks who have one purpose amongst others: to get us really drunk in the name of God. A pint of their ale looks like any other at a bar, only it comes with a hidden holy force of two to three times the amount of alcohol — perhaps because God intended us to embarrass ourselves by singing Journey songs on a karaoke mic sooner than later.

Belgian beer is very much ingrained in the country's gastronomy, so much that it's an ingredient in *carbonade flamande*, a Belgian beer-based stew of beef, onions, and savory spices. We are going to improvise this dish with *root* beer instead (hey, it's the closest they have at Carl's Jr.), so go pick up a pack of strong Trappist ales on your way home — it's going to take some pretty heavy inebriation to pass this dish's taste off as the real thing.

Ingredients (from Carl's Jr.):

2 Super Star Burgers (with bacon)
1 large order of French Fries
1 large order of Onion Rings
1 Side Salad (with low-fat balsamic vinaigrette)
1 large Root Beer
packets of ketchup and mustard

First, we need all the onions we can get, so **peel the breading off the onion rings** and then **dice the strands of white onions** found inside. There are more white onions in the burgers, so take those and **dice them** as well. Add all the onions to a saucepan and **sauté them** over a low heat until they start to sizzle.

Take the tomato slices from the burgers and finely **dice them down to a pulp**; add them to the saucepan. **Add more tomato via some ketchup**, and **squeeze in some mustard** as well. Add more liquid by **emptying in the packet of vinaigrette**; add more substance by way of meat: **cut the beef patties** into smaller chunks and **chop all the bacon**. Add those to the saucepan too.

Next, **pour in all the root beer**. Granted it's nothing like Belgian beer but at least it has the sugar that a real carbonade flamande recipe calls for (and then some). **Stir** as you **bring it to a boil**, and then **let it simmer** over a medium heat for 15–20 minutes until the beef gets tender.

Belgians are also known for their *frites*, so we are going to leave the French fries as is. With that said, we are ready to plate the meal: using a slotted spoon, **place some of the (root) beer-braised beef and onion stew on a plate**, leaving room on the side for the fries. **Chop some greens** from the side salad and **use it as a garnish**. *Voilà!*

TIPS FROM AN EMPTY JAR

If you can get away with passing this mock recipe off for the real thing, see if you can pass off some Eggos as Belgian waffles.

POUTINE VS. DISCO FRIES

Belgians may eat their fries with mayonnaise, but in French Canada, people eat it with gravy and melted cheese curds in what the Québécois call *poutine* — a dish so popular that even American-based fast food chains McDonald's, Burger King, and KFC have embraced it and put it on Canadian menus. However, poutine is oddly similar to the American dish known as "Disco Fries," served in the diners of New Jersey — fries topped with melted cheese and gravy.

I often have arguments with Canadians over which is better; they obviously side with their dish, and I, having spent my formative years in the Garden State, support the latter, arguing that in America we at least get to choose the type of cheese we want. (C'mon, *fuhgeddaboutit*.)

So which is fancier? Well obviously the word *"poutine"* intrinsically sounds classier with its Frenchy *"een"* syllable. The name "Disco Fries" is obviously the funkier of the pair, and does not contain the former's embarrassing *"poo"* syllable. Which tastes better? Well as the French say, *"à chacun son goût"* ("to each his own taste"); it's all subjective, and therefore the debate can go on and on forever. Ultimately, the conclusion is that no one really gives a shit about the petty arguments between Canadians and New Jerseyans, and the two parties should set their differences aside and embrace their common bond: that people love making fun of both of their accents.

FRENCH FRIED FANDOM

While we're on the subject of French fries, let's take a moment to pay tribute to the ones that many people, including yours truly, consider to be the *crème de la crème* of the fast food industry: the crispy golden ones from the Golden Arches of McDonald's. Sure other places have exceptional waffle-cut fries, steak fries, crinkle cuts, curly fries, and sweet potato ones, but when it comes judging the shoestring variety you can get from a drive-thru, many voted for McDonald's (except this girl I use to go out with in college, who actually preferred Burger King's fries instead. Needless to say, I shortly broke up with her after learning this.*)

While some may not agree that the best fries come from Mickey D's, they are in the minority; Zagat's Fast-Food Survey has declared McDonald's fries ahead of the pack three years in a row. Many eateries have tried to simulate qualities of their awesomeness, but never quite get it. When they're prepared right, there's no matching their unique taste, texture, and aroma — an enticing scent that has foreplay with your olfactory nerves even before you park your car. Occasionally, even some of the most health-conscious people can't resist, shunning everything on the McDonald's menu — except for those crispy fries.

So why are they so good? Is it the variety of potato they come from? The blend of oils they're fried in? Are they secretly laced with crack? Whatever it is that goes into their frying process or food laboratory engineering, it won't stop us fans from shoving more in our mouths. Do we care they're bad for us? Do we care that Morgan Spurlock showed us that they don't biodegrade like normal potatoes in that DVD extra of *Super Size Me*? Hell no! That's why we have molars and stomach bile. Plus, they're not *that* bad if we just have them on occasion, like we should with any fast food.

So McDonald's, keep doing what you're doing; your crispy fries were delicious before, they're delicious now, and they will stand the test of time. And I mean that quite literally; they will still be standing there for years, without any trace of mold or decomposition.

* She liked the formerly soggy BK fries before they switched over to a more respectable crispy recipe; it was definitely her, not me.

GRAS-FED STEAK AU POIVRE

✳ ✳ ✳ ✳ ✳

The gras *is always fatter on the other side.* *

As more people become educated about beef production, it's become more known that "grass-fed beef" is not just a label on a pack of sirloin steaks to drive up the cost; it's a designation to let us know that the cow whose loins became said steaks was raised on a natural diet. Grass-fed beef arguably tastes better because it's the flesh of cows that have eaten what cows were meant to eat: grass. Mother Nature didn't intend cows to be corralled in crowded commercial cattle lots and fed a high-starch diet of commodity corn; she meant for them to frolic in green pastures, like dancing Woodstock hippies. Actually, that is a bad analogy because it's not natural for cows to dance; they just meander around mooing, eating grass, and chewing cud. Plus they are really bad on their feet, particularly when kids go cow-tipping on the dance floor.

Here's a cow tip: buy grass-fed beef if you care about taste and can spare that extra dollar. Or just save some money, get the regular kind, and smother the beef in condiments, just like we will when making this faux version of the French dish, *steak au poivre*. In the end, the cow won't know the difference on how its diet determines its taste — because it's *dead*, of course.

Ingredients (from Fatburger):

1 large Fatburger (Kingburger) with lettuce and tomato; no cheese
1 order of Fat Fries
1 Vanilla Milk Shake
packets of salt
several packets of pepper

* *Sacré bleu! If you're rusty on your high school French (or forgot the meaning of Mardi Gras), "gras" is French for "fat."*

First, **scrape all the toppings off the Fatburger**, saving the tomatoes and the bigger clumps of lettuce; we'll use that as a side salad later. What's left on the bun is a big hunk of meat — half a pound of beef in fact — which is more or less the size and weight of a decent 8-ounce steak from a steakhouse. But let's make this Fatburger-turned-steak extra fatty by adding a pepper cream sauce.

Scoop some vanilla milk shake, along with some whipped cream topping, into a saucepan. It is obviously going to be sweet, so **add some salt packets** — just enough to mask the vanilla flavor. Then, **sprinkle in as many packets of pepper** that you can stand — the more the better; it's the *poivre* in our *au poivre* after all. **Stir well as it simmers** over a low heat.

For a side of potatoes, you can keep the steak-cut Fat Fries as is, or **blend them** into a mashed potatoes with a food processor. Add them to the side of your dinner plate, along with the makeshift side salad, as you complete the presentation: **place the steak on the plate**, then **smother it with the pepper cream sauce**. Forget how weird it is that you're taking a piece of dead cow and slathering it with a sugary concoction of its own milk. **Garnish it with more pepper** to really drown out the milk shake's sweetness. *Bon appétit!*

--- TIPS FROM AN EMPTY JAR ---

Adding pepper to a salty dish does not make it less salty, nor does adding salt to a peppery dish make it less peppery. (I learned this the hard way when I was a sneezy five-year-old.)

GRAS-FED STEAK AU POIVRE

WIENER SCHNITZEL FÄLSCHUNG

✽ ✽ ✽ ✽ ✽

Another dish for when you are sixteen going on seventeen... extra pounds.

So Burger King serves burgers, Pizza Hut serves pizza, and Taco Bell serves tacos. Ever wonder why the fast food chain Wienerschnitzel is actually called that when they don't actually serve *wiener schnitzel*, the Austrian dish of thinly cut meat that's breaded and fried? I mean, a lot of fast food is breaded and fried anyway, you think they would come to that conclusion, especially with a name like that. Perhaps they just wanted to reinterpret and tweak Austrian history for an American audience, much like Rodgers and Hammerstein did with *The Sound of Music*.

So how do you solve a problem like my Wienerschnitzel? Make wiener schnitzel using their available ingredients. Traditionally, wiener schnitzel is prepared with veal, which they haven't quite embraced — if not for the cost, then for the threat of animal rights protestors outside their doors with posters that rhyme (i.e. "Veal's no meal!"). Fortunately, not many negative words rhyme with "chicken," so we'll use poultry for the schnitzel instead. It's actually one of my favorite things.

Ingredients (from Wienerschnitzel):

4 Corn Dogs
1 order of French Fries
1 cup of water

PLUS: organic lemon and parsley (for garnish and an extra touch of irony)

Some variations of the Austrian dish call for chicken, which Wienerschnitzel has on the menu in one instance — at least parts of chicken anyway — in the processed chicken frank that resides inside their corn dog. Use a paring knife to **make an incision** in the side of each corn dog and **extract the chicken wieners** inside. Then take all the fried batter remains and **bake them** in a baking pan for about 15 minutes in a preheated oven at 400°F. When they're done, **let them cool** so that they get hard and crumbly, and then **grind them** down into bread crumbs using a food processor.

Meanwhile, **flatten the chicken franks** with a meat tenderizer mallet until they resemble thin, pink chicken cutlets. Then **coat them with a layer of the corn dog bread crumbs**. This mock escalope may tear apart easily, which is why we're going to just leave it looking pretty on a plate and not actually fry it.

For a side dish, we're going to serve the schnitzel not with noodles but with spaetzle. **Put all the fries in a food processor** and just **add a little bit of water** — enough to make the resulting mush a little clumpy. Then simply **form the little dumpling shapes** with your fingers.

When everything is ready, serve it not in a Wienerschnitzel box, but on a nice dinner plate. **Garnish it** with lemon wedges and parsley and you're done! *So long, farewell, auf Wiedersehen, good bite…*

FAST FOOD FOR THOUGHT

In 1913, the Coney Island Chamber of Commerce banned the term "hot dog" so the public wouldn't believe they were made from dogs. Thankfully, they were made from meat by-products — leftover organs, eyeballs, and bones of cows, pigs, and chickens — instead of our beloved canine friends. Whew, what a relief!

WIENER SCHNITZEL FÄLSCHUNG

HOW TO GIVE A VEGAN
A NICE CUP OF SHUT THE HELL UP

Many vegans are militant animal rights activists, so extreme that they think some vegetarians are assholes. They believe that humans in this day and age have no need to be dependent on (and thusly cruel to) other creatures of the animal kingdom — not only with meat, but any product derived from animals, may it be eggs, milk, cheese, or Coach leather handbags. As for fur coats, don't even think of getting them started. It's not going to be pretty.

Of course the downfall for vegans is that they don't get to eat all this delicious meat we have lying around, which is a shame. Alas, that is their choice — and besides, that means more meat for us! However, many vegans are self-righteous and preachy, and often talk meat-eaters' ears off, accusing them of being murderers. Don't get me wrong; not all vegans are like this. I have a few vegan friends, and they aren't constantly busting my balls for eating cheese or wearing a thin leather wristwatch band. However, if you find yourself cornered by an obnoxious vegan, here are a few things you can say when arguing back, so you can come off as a pompous dickwad too*:

- "I like animals as much as the next animal-lover, but I also like how good they taste."

- "All the extra estrogen from all that soy product is giving me man boobs."

- "What's more cruel, putting a cow out of its misery, or continually raping a cotton plant for those pairs of jeans?"

- "C'mon, even one of the little piggies had roast beef."

- "Hmm... seitan sure does sound a lot like *Satan*."

- "These chompers didn't evolve so I could chew on iron supplement pills."

- "It's called '*Eggs* Benedict,' not 'Tofu Substitute Benedict.'"

- "How can tempeh be that great if looks just as processed as Spam?"

- "You're right; meat is murder. But it's sweet, delicious, mouth-watering murder."

* *There's no guarantee you're going to win the argument; Hell hath no fury like a preachy vegan.*

BEEF STROG 'N OFF

✼ ✼ ✼ ✼ ✼

It's like playing Tetris with your taste buds.

Growing up during the final years of the Cold War, I knew Russia as the U.S.S.R., that bleak Soviet Union where people living under the system of Communism drank shots of vodka and stood on really long lines at the government store to buy toilet paper. On the world stage, they were America's adversary, a formidable competitor in the space race, Olympic figure skating, and boxing in *Rocky IV*.

Since the fall of the Soviet Union in 1991, the Ruskies are now America's comrades, joint capitalist pigs in free economies selling Pepsi, Levi's, and Big Macs. Russians can now choose from the menus of a variety of American fast food chains to warm up on a cold winter's day in Moscow. However, we are going to warm up with something more traditionally Russian, Beef Stroganoff — made entirely with food from a land where they once pointed their nukes.

**Ingredients
(from Steak 'n Shake):**

2 Grilled Portobello 'n Mushroom Steakburgers
1 Vanilla Milkshake
1 side order of Onion Rings
1 side order of Cottage Cheese

PLUS: organic dill weed (for garnish and an added touch of irony), and one shot of Russian vodka (as a chaser when you realize that this improvised dish doesn't taste very good)

First, **peel away the breading from the onion rings**, and **remove all the onions and mushrooms** from the steakburgers. **Chop the beef patties** into smaller bite-sized pieces. Then **sauté the beef, mushrooms, and onions** in a saucepan over a medium heat. There's just one key ingredient missing now, and we'll have to improvise.

> **TIPS FROM AN EMPTY JAR**
>
> *Stroganoff is traditionally made with sour cream, which isn't available at Steak 'n Shake. However, we've already added to the skillet the "steak" from the restaurant's name, so why not add the "shake?" (It's all in the name.)*

Spoon some sour cream-looking vanilla shake into the saucepan. The melted ice cream is obviously not sour, so **add 2 tablespoons of cottage cheese** to de-sweeten the mix. **Mush down the curds** with a spoon and **let the whole thing simmer** over a low heat.

To make the noodles, **break apart pieces of the bread** and **blend them down to dough** in a food processor with some cottage cheese whey. Take the resulting dough, **knead it**, and then **run it through a pasta maker** with a fettuccine attachment.

Plate your freshly-made fake pasta in the center of a fancy bowl, and then **smother it** with the simmering concoction. **Top it off with some ironic garnish** and there it is: Beef Strog 'N Off for a cold winter's day! Now **shoot some vodka** to numb its questionable taste. *Na zdorovia!*

WHOP PERGUIGNON

✻ ✻ ✻ ✻ ✻

"I just hate health food." –Julia Child

The 2009 chick flick *Julie & Julia* was partly based on the book *Julie and Julia: 365 Days, 524 Recipes*, which was an adaptation of the blog entitled "The Julie/Julia Project." In this blog, a bored but ambitious woman whose name I need not reveal*, attempts — and succeeds — in preparing every one of Julia Child's recipes in her original cookbook, *Mastering the Art of French Cooking*, within a year. But she didn't do it without a hitch; along the way, she faced some pretty treacherous obstacles, like squirming lobsters and self-induced hissy fits! Her story is paralleled to the life of Julia Child herself, who faced obstacles of her own, mainly the tops of door frames because she was freakishly tall.

Julia Child became an American icon with her savvy style, trilling voice, and above all, her talent for bringing French cooking to the American masses — a ruse to disguise a lot of fatty foods with a certain *je ne sais quoi*. Many traditional French dishes were made popular because of her, like *boeuf bourguignon*, the inspiration for this next recipe. If Mrs. Child were alive today, she would probably cringe at the thought of this mock dish made of items from Burger King — hell, anyone might cringe knowing what the ingredients are. Then again, Julia Child was an endorser of unhealthy food — many of her recipes called for lard or heaps of butter — so who am I know what she's thinking beyond the grave? In any case, this dish is sure going to look fancy.

So here's a "slight variation" of Mrs. Child's classic French recipe, which I'm sure that other woman would dare not try to prepare, throw a hissy fit, and blog about — but that doesn't mean you shouldn't try. Who knows? Maybe if you make it — and every other recipe in this *Fancy Fast Food* cookbook within a year — you too could get a movie deal.

---

* Hint: It's not "Julia."

Ingredients (from Burger King):

1 Whopper with bacon and mushrooms
1 Mushroom Swiss Steakhouse Burger
1 side order of French Fries
1 side order of Onion Rings
1 Garden Salad
2 bottles of "XXX" Vitaminwater
1 bottle of water
packets of salt, pepper, and ketchup

PLUS: organic parsley (for garnish and an added touch of irony)

First, **disassemble the burgers** to extract the ingredients we'll need: bacon, onions, mushrooms, burger patties, and buns. Then, using a paper towel, **dry off any oil, ketchup, or mayonnaise from the buns**, and **toast them** in a toaster (or conventional oven) until they become hard and crusty. Once they are cool to the touch, **grind the bread down into bread crumbs** with a food processor.

TIPS FROM AN EMPTY JAR

When choosing a burgundy-colored beverage to improvise the "bourguignon" part of this recipe, Burger King offers Vitaminwater in participating locations. A good vintage year for a good burgundy Vitaminwater is any one before 2010, when the FDA came after it for not actually being healthy.

Next, **cut the beef patties** into uneven square shapes, and then **slice the bacon into lardons** about a quarter-inch wide and an inch and a half long. **Sauté these small strips of bacon** in a saucepan for a bit and then **add in the beef. Stir the meats together** until they start to sizzle and then **pour in about two-thirds of a bottle of the Vitaminwater**. Once the beef has been moistened, take each piece with a pair of kitchen tongs and **bread it in the bread crumbs** you made earlier. (This will also help thicken the sauce, and soften the burger square edges so it looks more *au naturel*.) **Add in the baby carrots** from the garden salad, **a packet of ketchup, salt and pepper** to taste, and **stir**. Then cover the saucepan and **let it stew** for 20 minutes over a low heat.

Meanwhile, use a paring knife to **peel the breading off of the onion rings**. **Add the oniony pieces** to the mix of the other onions and mushrooms, and **rinse them** all in a colander. Then **sauté these mushrooms and onions** in a small skillet. Finally, **put the French fries**

in a food processor with some water and blend them until they become mashed potatoes.

Lastly, the plating: **place chunks of your beef stew on a fancy white plate. Top it with the sautéed onions and mushrooms**, and **garnish it** with chopped ironic parsley. **Serve some mashed potatoes** on the side, and then **pour some "bourguignon" gravy** from the saucepan over the meat and potatoes. Serve it with burgundy Vitaminwater in a wine glass and *voilà!* Now say *"Bon Appétit!"* with your best Julia Child impression!

TIPS FROM AN EMPTY JAR

Speaking of inspirational culinary chick flicks based on books, there's another one out there, starring another Julia (Julia Roberts): Eat Pray Love. *If you want to do things in that story on the cheap — just like making fancy meals with inexpensive fast food — just go get yourself a slice of pizza, rent a yoga DVD, and chant a couple of oms.*

94 FANCY MEATS

CELEBRITY CHEF MATCHING GAME

Can you match the celebrity chefs on the left with the personality traits on the right?

 A) Bobby Flay

1) loves to get naked and start the revolution

 B) Giada De Laurentiis

2) is BFF with Sara Lee and Duncan Hines

 C) Emeril Lagasse

3) believes chipotle mayonnaise makes anything better, even if it's on pancakes

 D) Rachael Ray

4) gets a little funky and spices like a fairy

 E) Jamie Oliver

5) has the most delicious recipe for type 2 diabetes

 F) Paula Deen

6) has heterosexual male viewers talking about melons, even if she's not making a melon salad

 G) Pat and Gina Neely

7) EVOO: Extremely Vexing On Occasion

 H) Sandra Lee

8) was inspired to make a catch phrase after watching Barney Rubble's son, Bamm-Bamm

ANSWERS: A:3, B:6, C:8, D:7, E:1, F:5, G:4, H:2

I think we're gonna need a bigger bowl.

FANCY SEAFOOD

✽ ✽ ✽ ✽ ✽

The marine food chain, in the simplest terms, goes as follows: tiny bacteria are eaten by algae, which are eaten by plankton and shrimp, which are eaten by little fish, which are eaten by medium-sized fish, which are eaten by sharks — which are captured on video so that we can watch them on TV during "Shark Week." But let's take it back down a few levels because *we* eat fish and shrimp too, along with crabs, lobsters, and shellfish (which sometimes feel like boogers in our mouths when we eat them raw and on the half shell).

Regardless, seafood will always be a part of our land-dwelling food chain, as long as nutritionists keep raving like lunatics about the health benefits of the omega-3 fatty acids found in fish. However, when we deep-fry seafood and load it with tartar sauce, all those healthy fats are outnumbered by unhealthy ones, and we might as well be eating greasy fried chicken. Then again, fish has unique tastes that chicken will never have — whether it's fried or not — so thankfully it's here to stay. That's a good thing because TV shows about big chickens don't quite have the same on-air appeal; "Rooster Week" just doesn't have as much punch as "Shark Week," and "Cock Week" is just plain inappropriate.

LONG JOHN CEVICHE

✳ ✳ ✳ ✳ ✳

Avast, me hearties!

Aye, before them corporate scallywags tried to make Long John Silver's all posh 'n chips, there'd be no fast food chain that'd make ye want to talk like a pirate more. Them buccaneers used to be havin' all hands on deck when hoistin' the Jolly Roger, pillagin' 'n plunderin', and sailin' the seven seas to catch shrimp 'n fish for all ye scurvy dogs, from the depths o' Davy Jones' locker. *Aye,* we'll be classin' up their ol' pirate-themed fried seafood grub, me bucko, and handsomely style a fancy chum dish that'll be appeasin' to the eye of any landlubber. *Yo ho ho!* So stop swabbin' the deck, put down yer booty, and get ye o'er to the galley, or else ye be walkin' the plank! *Yarrrr...*

Ingredients (from Long John Silver's):

1 Two Fish and Eight Shrimp Platter
1 side order of Corn
1 side order of Coleslaw
packets of vinegar
plenty o' packets of lemon juice

PLUS: a strip of organic lime zest (for garnish and a touch o' landlubbin' irony)

> **FAST FOOD FOR THOUGHT**
>
> *During International Talk Like A Pirate Day (September 19th), the average person can only maintain a maximum three minutes of consecutive pirate slang.*

First, **peel the breading off the fried fish** and **cut the fillets** into small bite-sized morsels. Peel the breading off the eight shrimp but only **cut off the shelled tails** of *five* of them; **save three whole ones** for garnish. **Chop the five peeled shrimp** into smaller pieces and then **mix them in a bowl** with the pieces of fish.

Rinse the coleslaw in a colander, and **strain the corn** in a strainer. **Add both of those to the bowl of seafood.** Then **add in plenty of lemon juice**, along with **a little vinegar** from the packets. **Mix all the ingredients well**, making sure the citric acid of lemon marinates everything. Then **let it chill in the refrigerator** for at least a half an hour.

Aye, it be time fer de platin'... **Spoon out enough of the chilled ceviche to fill a martini glass** just below the rim and then **garnish the top with the three remaining shrimp. Curl and add the strip of lime zest** for a little color, and now you have a gourmet ceviche that looks good enough to eat. *Shiver me timbers!* Don't forget to ring the bell if ye did well!

AHOY, MATEYS!

Before Long John Silver's classy rebranding, participating locations offered cardboard pirate hats, so you could look like a pirate. But did you know those hats could make *anything* look like a pirate?

dalmatians

bowling balls

cactuses that look like they have swords and parrots on their shoulders

GUMBO D-LUXE

✳ ✳ ✳ ✳ ✳

D-lightful and D-licious.

Fast food chain Captain D's Seafood Kitchen may have originated in Donelson, Tennessee, but I'm going to give props to New Orleans instead with this mock Cajun seafood recipe. Let's face it; New Orleans has been through enough in recent years, with Hurricane Katrina, the BP oil spill, and all the paparazzi photographers trying to get a picture of transplanted resident Sandra Bullock with her kid. Fortunately, things have gotten better for The Big Easy and its economy since those disasters struck. Mardi Gras attendance is up, which means many more visitors are spending money at local businesses on not only booze, but on regional cuisine — including gumbo, the okra-based African stew that bayou country has embraced and made its own.

However, if you're not quite ready for New Orleans and its drunken Mardi Gras revelers flashing their nips for beads and puking their heads off all over Bourbon Street, here's a simple gumbo recipe you can make at home with takeout fast food, so you can pretend you're there. But be warned: if you're one of those people with food texture issues who gags at the sliminess of some foods — cooked okra often feels like slugs in your mouth — you might just simulate the vomiting too.

Ingredients (from Captain D's):

1 Deluxe Seafood Platter, which includes:
2 Fried Fish Fillets
4 Fried Shrimp
2 Stuffed Crab Shells
a side of Green Beans
a side of Coleslaw
Hush Puppies
2 extra sides of Fried Okra
1 cup of water
packets of hot sauce

PLUS: organic parsley (for garnish and a touch of irony)

First, **skin the breading off the fish fillets**, **chop them** into smaller bite-sized pieces, and put them in a saucepan. Then, **peel the breading off the shrimp** and add them to the fish morsels. Use a spoon to scoop out and **add in the seafood stuffing** from the crab shells as well. So far the pot is full of seafood, so let's add the vegetables — most importantly, the okra. **Peel the breading off all the fried okra** and toss them in. Also **add the coleslaw**. Then **stir in the water** and **bring it all to a boil**.

TIPS FROM AN EMPTY JAR

Imitation crab meat is made out of a paste of puréed whitefish. If you're ever hard up for fake crab, cut out the middle man and just blend some fishsticks in a blender.

To thicken the broth, **crumble in some hush puppies** to the stew. If you'd like to *kick it up a notch*, **add the hot sauce**. **Stir well**, **cover it**, and **let it simmer** over a low heat for 15–20 minutes.

When all the ingredients are fused together, **ladle out the gumbo** into a serving bowl and **garnish it** with some ironic parsley. *Hooo-weee!* Now it's time for some good eatin'!

FAST FOOD FOR THOUGHT

Emeril Lagasse once kicked it up a notch so hard that Pluto was ejected from our solar system. Cosmic BAM!

GUMBO D-LUXE

SEAFOOD FAUXSOTTO

❊ ❊ ❊ ❊ ❊

You say "risotto," I say "ris-ah-tto"... Let's call the whole thing off.

Celebrity chef Mario Batali once had this to say about risotto: *"Ow! WTF?"* This is of course me paraphrasing his words during an incident he once spoke of in a recorded interview, when he was hit in the chest by a hot pan of risotto. The pan was thrown by none other than acclaimed British chef Marco Pierre-White during one of his kitchen tantrums, when he bitched about the risotto not being right. A bewildered Batali left the kitchen shortly thereafter but not before sabotaging all the sauces with handfuls of salt.

To any foodie, that's quite an interesting anecdote — Handfuls of salt... That'll show *him*! — but to anyone else, it's pretty lame. I mean, really? Is that all you got, Batali? Come on, I was itching to hear it escalate into a *real* celebrity chef battle or better yet, an *Animal House*-style food fight. You could have at least poured cream over Marco's head or something. (Now *that's* something I'd pay to see at a celebrity chef forum.)

Anyway, here's my mock recipe for a faux risotto that will admittedly *not* be worthy of any celebrity chef's approval, which means I should probably keep my guard up. Just be warned: if a hot pan of risotto comes into contact with my chest, you better brace yourself, because it's going to be *on* like *Donkey Kong*...

Ingredients
   (from Rubio's):
1 World Famous Fish Taco
1 Grilled Mesquite Shrimp Taco
1 Grilled Mahi-Mahi Taco
1 Grilled Portobello & Poblano Taco
1 Grilled Veggie Burrito (with no black beans or chimichurri sauce; sour cream on the side)
1 large order of Rice
1 extra sour cream
4 condiment cups of cilantro and onion salsa

104 FANCY SEAFOOD

SUPER MARIO (BATALI) BROS.

Speaking of Donkey Kong, did you ever realize that if you thickened Mario Batali's moustache, put him in plumber clothes, and gave him a bad stereotypical Italian accent, he could go around saying, "It's-a me! Mario!"? It's not like he doesn't already deal with mallets or big mushrooms in the kitchen. Maybe he could power-up with some portobellos next time and fight back during any future risotto attacks by celebrity chefs — or big turtles for that matter.

First, take the contents of three of the four little cups of **cilantro and onions**, and **sauté them** in a skillet. Then, **stir in all the rice** over a low heat.

We're going to add two types of fish to our mixture: the **grilled mahi-mahi**, and for posterity's sake, the **beer-battered fish** inside the World Famous Fish Taco. For the latter, **skin the batter off** and then **chop both kinds of fish** into smaller pieces. Add them to the skillet and **stir**.

This shall be a creamy risotto, so **fold in all of the sour cream**. It's also going to contain portobello mushrooms like any good risotto, so **pick them out** from the grilled veggie burrito and the portobello and poblano taco. **Chop them** and then add them to the skillet. **Mix everything together** over a low heat.

Lastly, the plating: **scoop some fauxsotto into a fancy bowl** and then **garnish the center with the shrimp** from the grilled mesquite shrimp taco. **Top it off** with some leftover cilantro. *Presto!* Now watch out for flying pans!

--- FAST FOOD FOR THOUGHT ---

Originally I was going to call this recipe "Rubotto" — a combination of "Rubio's" and "risotto" — but I didn't want people to get mad at me for getting the '80s band Styx' "Mr. Roboto" stuck in their heads. Or did mentioning that tidbit do the trick? Domo arigato...

106 FANCY SEAFOOD

SPICY CHICKEN MOCKI SUSHI

✷ ✷ ✷ ✷ ✷

Well blow me down.

In what is now a pop culture story for the ages, former pop star Jessica Simpson once said to her then pop star husband Nick Lachey, "Is this chicken what I have, or is this fish? It says Chicken by the Sea." This was during a televised conversation on their MTV reality show *Newlyweds: Nick and Jessica*, when Ms. Simpson was confused about her Chicken of the Sea brand tuna, whether or not it was actually made of chicken. This little conversation was pounced by the media, which exploded into a frenzy of jokes on every late night talk show, and even a skit on *Saturday Night Live*, in which Jessica Simpson herself poked fun of the incident. This not only did publicity wonders for her, but for the guys in the PR department at Chicken of the Sea headquarters, who were quick to capitalize on the stupidity of blondes.

To be fair, there is some basis in Jessica Simpson's confusion; cooked tuna sometimes *does* have a similar color and texture to chicken, particularly the solid albacore variety. So let's capitalize on this ambiguity and try to pass off chicken as fish in this next exercise of Fancy Fast Food styling.

Ingredients (from Popeyes):

1 Two-Piece Spicy Fried Chicken Dinner (breast and wing)
1 Loaded Chicken Wrap
1 Biscuit
1 side order of Coleslaw
1 large Coke (no ice)
1 large order of Red Beans and Rice
packets of hot sauce

PLUS: organic wasabi paste (for garnish and an added touch of irony)

> **FAST FOOD FOR THOUGHT**
>
> *I once demonstrated this mock sushi recipe for Rachael Ray on her daytime talk show. The chopstick holder in the shape of a funny little naked lady (shown in the previous picture) was considered too racy for a morning audience and was censored by Ms. Ray's people — even though the following segment involved female masturbation.*

This recipe calls for Coca-Cola reduction, so first **pour half the cup into a nonstick skillet. Bring it to a boil** and let it reduce as you prepare the other items.

Unwrap the Loaded Chicken Wrap and **unload the chicken tender inside**. As best as you can, **separate the rice from the red beans** remaining in the wrap and place the two items into two separate bowls. In each of these bowls, **add the rice and the red beans** from the large side order respectively. Then **rinse the rice** in a colander and pick out any remaining red beans. **Dry the rice** in a paper towel and let it air out for a while. Now that you have an empty wrap, **rinse it and cut off its rounded edges** to make a rectangle.

Next, **cut the tip off the chicken tender** about two inches, then **skin and bone the rest**, along with the chicken breast and wing. Using the biggest masses of white meat from the chicken tender and chicken breast, **cut out four little rectangular slabs of chicken**, each about the size of a domino tile. Then take all the remaining chicken and **chop it finely. Add the chopped chicken** into the bowl of red beans, then **add hot sauce** from the packets to your liking. **Mix it all** into a consistent paste.

Once the Coke has been reduced to a thick, dark syrup, place the wrap into the saucepan to **dye it a dark brown**. When enough of the syrup has infused the wrap, **place it face down on a bamboo sushi roller**. Then **add a layer of rice** on top of that, followed by a **strip of the chicken/bean mix** in the center of the wrap. **Roll the wrap** into the shape of a maki roll, **cut off the ends**, and then **cut the roll** into six equal parts. A lot of the syrup coloring may have rubbed off during this process, so **reapply the coloring** to each piece with a pastry brush as needed.

Cut the edges off the buttermilk biscuit and then **cut it in half** to make two rectangular pieces. Slice those two pieces laterally to make four rectangular pieces of about equal size. **Place the four pieces of chicken** on each of the four biscuit pieces.

Finally, the plating: **place the six "mocki" roll pieces on the platter**. In one of them, **insert the tip of the chicken tender**, standing it upwards so that it resembles a shrimp tempura roll. **Accentuate the center of each roll piece** with a bean and more hot sauce. Place the four chicken and biscuit "sushi" pieces onto the platter, then **drizzle and glaze them with more of the Coke reduction. Drain and rinse the coleslaw** in a colander and then use it as an additional garnish, along with a dab of ironic wasabi paste. You're done! Now serve it with chopsticks. *Douzo meshiagare!*

BAJA BOUILLABAISSE

❋ ❋ ❋ ❋ ❋

Twist your tongue on this.

Bouillabaisse is a savory seafood stew prominent in the provinces of Provence, a culinary classic from the seaside city of Marseille. (Try saying that three times fast.) Not only can it be described in alliterative tongue twisters, but "bouillabaisse" is a word that just sounds fancy, doesn't it? Say it out loud: "I'll have the *bouillabaisse*." See, you sound like a total food snob now.

The most discerning food snob knows that best bouillabaisse is made with only the *freshest* seafood, but since we are going to play by our own rules and only source ingredients from the realm of fast food chains, we'll go to the chain that labels their food as such (even if it's inspired by Mexico and not France): Baja *Fresh*. With their available sea-faring fast food fare, we're going to boil up a "Baja Bouillabaisse" that will not only appease the Fancy Fast Food kitchen's affection for alliterations, but entice the eyes — and maybe even tantalize a taste bud or two. (My twisted tongue actually enjoyed the taste of this one enough to save the leftovers for lunch the next day.)

Ingredients (from Baja Fresh Mexican Grill):

1 BFF Fire-grilled Burrito (with langostino lobster)
3 Original Baja Tacos (with grilled shrimp)
3 Mahi-Mahi Tacos (grilled)
1 Garden Salad
1 Chicken Tortilla Soup (without charbroiled chicken)
4 condiment cups of pico de gallo
1 condiment cup of chopped cilantro

First, **pour the soup into a saucepan**; this will be the savory stock of our seafood stew, even if it's based on terrestrial poultry. **Add tomatoes and onions** to this base via the pico de gallo — but **don't throw away the condiment cups** just yet since we'll get creative with them later. **Bring it to a boil** and then **let it simmer** over a low heat.

Next, the main ingredients: the seafood. For fish, we have the strips of grilled mahi-mahi from the tacos; **add those to the saucepan** and **let them stew** until they are tender enough to **cut into smaller chunks** with a mixing spoon. Also **add in the grilled shrimp** from the other tacos. Then **pick the pieces of "lobster" meat** out of the burrito and add it to the saucepan. Cover and **let it simmer** over a low heat for 5–10 minutes.

--- FAST FOOD FOR THOUGHT ---

When fast food chains offer "lobster," usually they are referring to the "langostino lobster," which isn't even a part of the true lobster family; it's a two-inch crustacean that's more like a hermit crab. "Langostino" is actually Spanish for prawn (which isn't in the true lobster family either), but somehow the name got adopted and allowed by the FDA (possibly for its nifty alliteration), making the controversial crustacean the long-lost Spanish orphan that somehow acquired the elite Lobster family name — sort of like a third-world baby hitting the Hollywood adoption jackpot.

--- TIPS FROM AN EMPTY JAR ---

Sally may sell seashells by the seashore, but you can get by with the Baja Bouillabaisse without her business on the beach.

Images of a real bouillabaisse often include the shells of clams or mussels, but we'll improvise with a little creativity and the empty condiment cups. Using a pair of kitchen shears, **cut the black condiment cups** along the sides to make long oval shapes. When they curl, they will resemble mussel shells — especially when you cleverly position them in a serving bowl. But first, **add them to the saucepan** so they get immersed in the stock; this will help prevent them from looking like plastic. (Don't worry; they won't melt.)

Finally, the plating: use a ladle to **transfer the seafood stew into a fancy bowl**. **Place the mock mussel shells** in and around the morsels of fish and seafood, and then **garnish the top** with the chopped cilantro. *Voilà!*

112 FANCY SEAFOOD

QUENELLES-O-FISH

✻ ✻ ✻ ✻ ✻

Hook, line, and sinker.

If you fish around the 'net* and do a little research, you can find the answer to the question of just what is inside a McDonald's Filet-O-Fish: actual *fish*. It is a white fish, usually pollock or hoki, commercially fished from cold, deep waters. The other questions surrounding the famous fish sandwich are: If it's really fish, then why is it square? Doesn't the square creature found under the sea live in a pineapple and wear equally square pants?

You can fish around the 'net for that answer too, but the real issue is, who cares if it's square? Sure it's not the natural shape of fish, but neither are sticks, and those are everywhere. Still, some food snobs out there may scoff at those peculiar shapes — but it's not like there isn't another oddly shaped fish dish out there, one that Julia Child called "a delicate triumph of French cooking": *quenelles de poisson*.

Quenelles, like Filet-O-Fish squares, are also typically made from white fish, but have no right angles; they have an oval, un-fish-like shape, similar to eggs. And when you lay them down on a plate without any garnish and add a creamy sauce, they too look peculiar; they sort of look like little brains or testicles. So, which is more questionable: fast food fish squares or delicate testicle shapes on a plate? Now *there's* a question for you. Try fishing around the 'net for the answer to that one — or just see for yourself in your kitchen...

Ingredients (from McDonald's):

4 Filet-O-Fish Sandwiches
  (for two pairs of "testicles")
1 Side Salad (with ranch
  dressing)
1 small beverage of your choice
packets of ketchup

* *Pun intended.*

First, use a small spoon to **transfer all the tartar sauce** from the filet squares and upper buns into a mixing bowl. The tartar sauce will serve as the creamy panade that will bind the fish together.

Next, skin the four filets: use a sharp knife to **cut the edges off the squares** first, and then gently **skin the top and bottom off** by gliding your knife sideways. What you'll have left are flaky pieces of white fish; **add them to the mixing bowl**.

Use a fork to **mush the fish with the tartar sauce**. Mix it up until it's all thoroughly combined into a consistent paté, and then start forming the quenelles. Take one dinner spoon in one hand to **scoop out a dollop of the mixture**, and then use another dinner spoon in your other hand, inverted over the first one, to **mold the oval shape** of the quenelle. Gently **glide the upper spoon forward and backward** so that the surface of the quenelle smoothens out. Then flip both spoons so the quenelle is transferred to the second spoon, and then repeat the shaping process for the other half. When you've repeated this over to make four or five quenelles, **place each of them on a fancy plate**.

For the sauce, we'll make a pinkish cream sauce to simulate the crevette sauce they serve in Lyon, the city in central France known for fish quenelles. **Pour all of the ranch dressing in a beaked measuring cup** and then **add just enough ketchup to give it a pinkish hue**. Mix it well and then use it generously to **pour over each of the quenelles. Garnish with a leafy green** from the side salad and *voilà!* A fancy, fishy dish as peculiar as the fish it came from. Or is it? You be the judge of that.

ONE FISH, TWO FISH, JESUS FISH, JEW FISH

If you have a Jewishly trained eye, you may have noticed that these "Quenelles-O-Fish" look oddly similar to those jarred fish balls you see in the Manischewitz section of the grocery store. That's right, during Shabbat dinner you could probably pass these off as Fancy Fast Food's mock recipe for "Gefilte-O-Fish!" Then again, who are we kidding? That wouldn't be kosher!

However, this does bring up the question: what is the difference between gefilte fish and quenelles? They are both prepared in a similar way, and with similar ingredients. Perhaps they were just created at the same time in France, but the word *"quenelle"* dominated because it was in French — and therefore inherently sounded fancier. Also, French Catholics have outnumbered French Jews for centuries.

Speaking of Catholicism, have you noticed that many American fast food chains ramp up their seafood and fish selections during the Catholic season of Lent, the few weeks before Easter? This is so they can capitalize on the Catholic law forbidding the consumption of meat on those Fridays, when practicing non-vegetarian Catholics typically eat fish for protein instead of meat. Maybe the Pope just *really* likes Filet-O-Fish sandwiches — so much that he made it a rule.

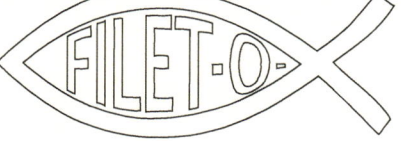

Yo quiero tortellini.

FANCY PASTA & NOODLES

✸ ✸ ✸ ✸ ✸

"Pasta" is simply Italian for "paste," which is odd because when you eat paste in America, you're that weird kid in kindergarten class. Thankfully we've adopted the word "pasta" to distinguish it from paste; we mean it to define a different, less adhesive substance that's more like dough. Pasta, in its most raw definitive form, is nothing more than water and flour mixed together and extruded into different shapes — and these shapes are the easiest way to explain how texture is an important part of the eating experience. You can pour a jar of Prego on any rearrangement of pasta, may it be spaghetti, linguine, penne, rigatoni, cellatani, farfalle, or angel hair — all different shapes made of the same stuff — and yet because of the way it feels in your mouth, it is a completely different thing. The variations of different pastas and sauces are limitless; master chefs are always coming up with different combinations of tastes and textures — most notably the exquisite dish of macaroni, *ragù Bolognese*, and preservatives in celebrity chef Boyardee's recipe for Beefaroni.

Let's do some rearranging of tastes and textures ourselves, using ingredients from fast food joints. So get your pasta maker out — or your old Play-Doh Spaghetti Factory playset — and get to it. Who's the weird kid now?

TACOBELLINI

✻ ✻ ✻ ✻ ✻

Think outside the taco.

You won't find any bells to ring at Taco Bell (like they've had at Long John Silver's), for the origin of the "bell" in "Taco Bell" didn't come from the bell in its logo, or from the fact that you hear a big "dong" sound at the end of a TV commercial. Taco Bell was partly named after its founder Glen Bell Jr., who had quite the American life being a U.S. Marine-turned-fast food mogul. I guess nothing says "Welcome back to America from killing the Japs in WWII" than making a couple of tacos, huh?

According to TacoBell.com, Mr. Bell was quite the inventor too, having invented the pre-formed hard taco shell in 1951, so that Americans could prepare Mexican food faster — even though any Mexican will tell you that real tacos are always served with *soft* tortillas, and without guacamole that comes out of a caulking gun. But there's no argument that Mr. Bell had the spirit of American invention, with ideas that were, as they say, "outside the bun." We're going to take that ingenuity a step further by thinking outside his hard taco shell and making a tortellini dish.

Ingredients (from Taco Bell):

2 Burrito Supremes (with beef)
1 Beef Soft Taco
packets of Border Sauce

PLUS: organic parsley (for garnish and an extra touch of irony)

118 FANCY PASTA & NOODLES

Carefully unwrap the Burrito Supremes and soft taco—making sure the tortilla doesn't tear — and **extract their fillings** into a mixing bowl. Carefully **rinse off each of the tortillas** and then briefly **steam them in a steamer** so they become soft and moist. Then lay each tortilla on a cutting board and **cut circles** in it using a small circular cookie cutter, or simply an empty tin can measuring about 2 ½ inches in diameter.

Mix the fillings well and then **spoon a small amount** in each small tortilla circle. **Fold it in half** and then **pinch it into a tortellini shape** — the moisture should keep it sticky enough for it to stay put. **Repeat this process** until you run out of tortilla circles. As for the sauce, simply **cut and pour all the hot sauce** from the packets into a spouted measuring cup.

Lastly, the plating: **pile the tortellini** in the center of a fancy plate, then generously **drizzle the sauce** over the tortellini. Garnish with ironic parsley and serve. ¡*Buen provecho!*

OTHER USES FOR THAT GUACAMOLE CAULKING GUN

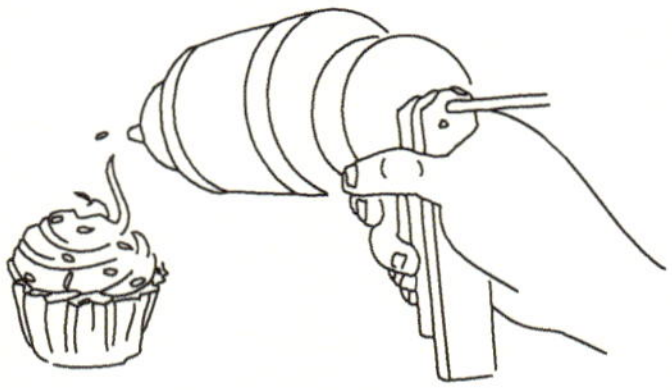

decorating cupcakes

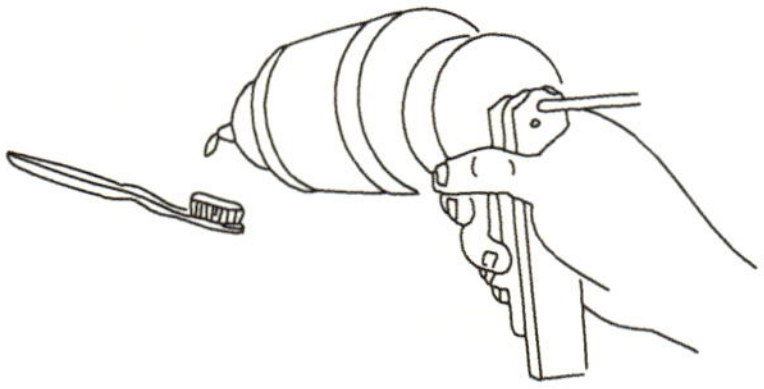

toothpaste

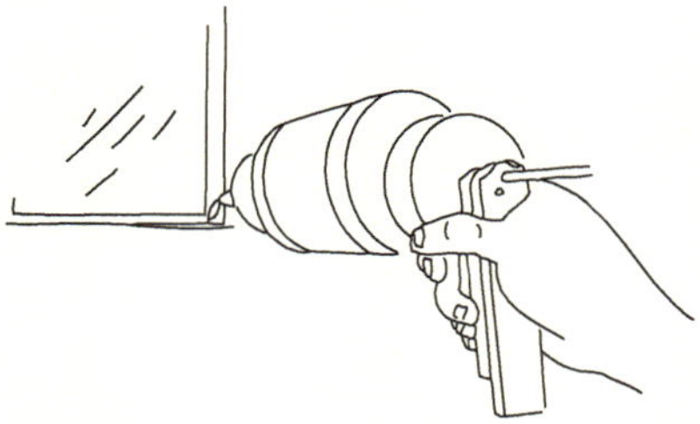

insolating your window frames with avocado

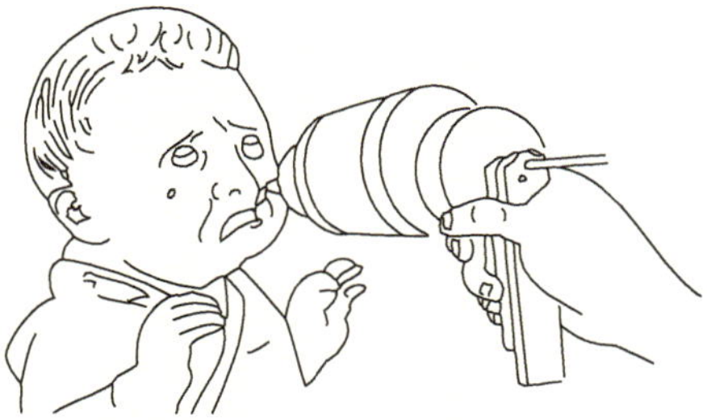

feeding a baby

TACOBELLINI 119

DEL SPAGHETTI ARRABBIATA

✻ ✻ ✻ ✻ ✻

A culinary lesson in anger management.

Arrabbiata is Italian for "angry," which makes the sauce in this next recipe one pissed off marinara. And who can blame it? After all these years, someone *still* hasn't fixed those lopsided stairs in the Tower of Pisa.

In actuality, the "anger" in arrabbiata sauce is derived from spices — specifically from red pepper flakes — and the more you add, the more flavorful and zesty it becomes. Metaphorically speaking, it also becomes more infuriated. Sure, add a pinch of spice and it's slightly annoyed about tax hikes and the economy, but add in a heaping tablespoon and that sauce is going to be mad as hell and it's not going to take it anymore!

So when making an arrabbiata sauce — authentic or otherwise (i.e., with hot sauce packets) — remember to turn up the heat and spice it up, since that's the way it was intended to be. Make it angry; it's one case when you would like something when it's angry. Just don't add *too* much or else the red sauce will turn green when it bulges out of its shirt and transforms into the Incredible Hulk.

Ingredients (from Del Taco):

1 Del Classic Chicken Burrito (or any burrito without rice, sour cream, and guacamole)
1 order of Jalapeño Rings
1 cup of water
packets of assorted hot sauces
packets of ketchup

PLUS: organic basil leaves (for garnish and an added touch of irony)

First, unwrap the burrito and **empty the filling into a saucepan** with a little bit of water, and **place it over a medium heat.** Next, **add plenty of ketchup and hot sauce** from the packets — as many as you can stand. To make it even hotter, **chop up some jalapeño rings** and add them to the mix. **Let the sauce simmer** for 10 minutes, stirring occasionally.

To make the pasta, **rinse the tortilla** and then **cut the sides off** so it has the width of a pasta cutter. **Crank the tortilla through** the pasta cutter's spaghetti attachment and **pile the resulting pasta** in the center of a fancy white plate, and then **add the arrabbiata sauce** on top. **Garnish** with ironic basil leaves and *presto!* Now don't get mad at me!

SOME LIKE IT HOT, SOME LIKE IT ASS BLASTING

I like spicy foods just as much as the next person, but I also like still feeling a sensation in my lips and stomach lining. However, perhaps I am in the minority because there are tons of different hot sauces out there on the market of varied levels of hotness — more than Del Taco's Mild, Del Scorcho, and Del Inferno:

Spiciness	Examples	Characteristics
mild	Del Taco's Mild Sauce, Taco Bell's Mild Border Sauce	not even on the radar of any spicy food connoisseur, but for the individual who usually can't handle any kind of spicy food, this is the first step to growing a pair
medium hot	Frank's Red Hot, Cholula	has a savory tang and just enough spice to heat things up a little bit, but not quite enough to put some hair on your chest
hot	Tabasco, Sriracha sauce	aids in sinus congestion during flu season; aids in ulcer construction during the other seasons
extra hot	Ass Blaster*, Rectum Ripper*, Sphincter Shrinker*	does things to your bowels that you didn't even know they could endure; also rips apart rectums and shrinks sphincters (but that's a given)
volcanic	Atomic Wings' Nuclear, Colon Blow Red Habanero Enema*	may require the use of a pencil or a wooden stick to bite down on while you deal with the pain; aids in constipation using liquid hot magma
the fires of Hell	Mad Dog 22 Midnight Special Pepper Extract*	will burn a fire trail down your esophagus if you can even make it passed your throat — and if you're not busy hyperventilating from all the crying; can be used as natural pepper spray

I am not making this up; see for yourself at www.HotSauce.com.

CHINESE CHECKERS CHOW MEIN

❋ ❋ ❋ ❋ ❋

Ancient Chinese secret, eh?

In the thirteenth century, Italian explorer Marco Polo set off on an overland expedition to the Far East, where he learned about a great many Asian things that he brought back to the Western World — mostly, pirated DVDs. He has often been credited with introducing the concept of Chinese noodles to the Italians, who then added sauce on it and called it "spaghetti" — with an Italian accent and expressively manic hand gestures, of course. Italian historians have argued (also with manic hand gestures) that their fellow paisans came up with noodles all by themselves, without the stories of Marco Polo's travels in Asia. Meanwhile, the Chinese people still claim to have invented them first — at least that's what the government told them.

Whether you side with the Italians or Chinese is up to you, but ultimately we should all set our differences aside and just credit Marco Polo for being the namesake of that blindfolded hide-and-seek game that kids play in the pool. (*"Marco...!"*) So forget about the debate of where noodles came from; we're going to make them out of hamburger buns. (*"...Polo!"*)

**Ingredients
 (from Checkers/Rally's):**

2 Big Bufords (with no cheese)
1 medium Coke
2 small cups of Asian Kick Sauce

First, **disassemble the burgers** and **separate the patties** from the toppings. **Tear the buns into smaller pieces** and **put them in a food processor**, **add in about 3 tablespoons of Coke**, and then **blend it** into a dough. (The dark color of Coke will give the dough come color.)

Knead the dough and then **roll it flat** with a rolling pin. **Trim the edges** so the dough fits into a pasta cutter with the spaghetti attachment, and then **cut it into strands** of doughy chow mein. (Alternatively, you could use a pasta maker that extrudes noodles from wads of dough.)

Bias-cut the beef patties (that means diagonally) and **dice the tomatoes**. **Rinse the mayonnaise** off all the vegetable toppings. Then, **stir fry the sliced beef, vegetables, and noodles** in a wok until it's all fused together — be careful not to stir too hard or the noodles will clump back into wads of dough. For an added Asian kick, **add the Asian Kick Sauce**. Finally, plate the meal and serve it with chopsticks and a fortune cookie!

FAST FOOD FOR THOUGHT

What's the deal with the game Chinese Checkers? How is it checkers, but somehow "Chinese" when it's played on a board in the shape of the Star of David? I thought the game that unified old Chinese women and old Jewish women was mahjong...

UNFORTUNATE FORTUNES

Here's a list of fortunes you may never read from a fortune cookie ("...in bed."):

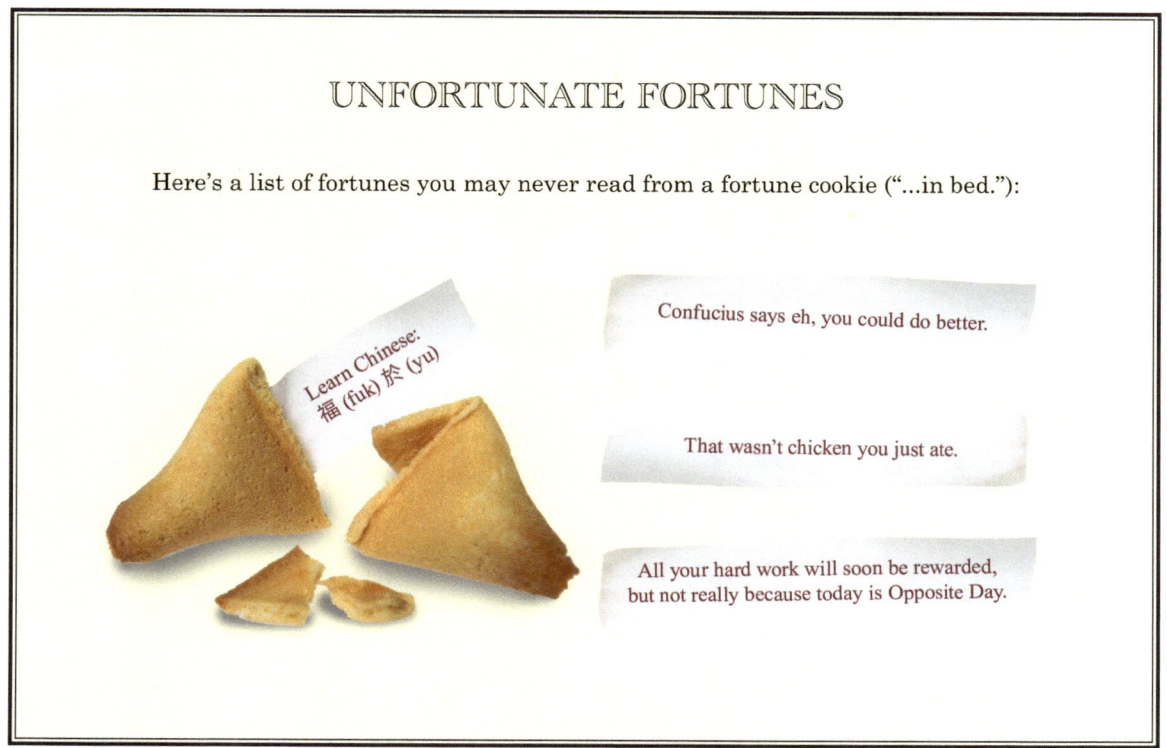

Learn Chinese: 福 (fuk) 於 (yu)

Confucius says eh, you could do better.

That wasn't chicken you just ate.

All your hard work will soon be rewarded, but not really because today is Opposite Day.

FIVE-DOLLAR FARFALLE

✳ ✳ ✳ ✳ ✳

Jared better dress up for this one.

When the eponymous Fancy Fast Food blog launched on the Internet, some readers were inspired because these fancy-looking food transformations could be done to impress chicks — without breaking their budgets. These enlightened readers, I assume, were mostly single dudes sitting on their couches in their underwear, watching sports or playing Halo next to piles of empty bottles and boxes of cold pizza crusts — all while waiting for the next unemployment check to come in.

Sure, dude, you could make a fancy farfalle dish out of a five-dollar footlong at Subway like in this next mock recipe, but that's just *one* step in trying to woo the ladies on the cheap. For one, clean up the place if you're going to invite a classy lady over for dinner, no matter where the ingredients come from. Put away your video games, hide your porn, and stick a beer bottle cap under that uneven table leg. Then clean yourself up; put on a nice shirt and spray it with some Febreeze if you can't afford to do a load of laundry. And while you're at it, it should go without say that no matter how taxing it may seem, you should probably put some pants on too — especially when you're going out to get the ingredients. The signs may say "No Shirt, No Shoes, No Service," but trust me, they might not serve you without pants on either.

Ingredients (from Subway):

- 1 Subway $5 Footlong with chicken breast on Italian bread with double tomatoes, olives, green peppers, and onions
- 2 condiment cups of red wine vinegar dressing
- 1 bottle of water

126 Fancy Pasta & Noodles

First, **take all the ingredients out of the Italian bread**, and put them aside. Then **break pieces of the bread into a food processor**, **add some water**, and **blend it down** until it turns back into dough. **Lay a sheet of wax paper** onto a flat surface and **knead the dough** on top. Then, using a rolling pin, **roll a small piece of the dough flat** on the non-stick surface. You should have enough flattened dough to **cut out a serrated square** using a

SPEAKING OF PANTS...

You've all heard the story: Jared Fogle, former fatty weighing in at 425 pounds, had this crazy idea to lose weight after every other diet failed: eat nothing but two low-fat Subway sandwiches a day. His idea worked, and in less than a year he shed off over 200 pounds, which finally gave him hope — and the ability to see his own feet.

Jared subsequently went on to become the spokesperson for Subway — many calling him "The Subway Guy" — and was a symbol of hope for the obese. He appeared in commercials and on tours explaining his tremendous weight loss, illustrating it with his former 60-inch waist pants — a gimmick that lasted in Jared's campaign for nearly a decade. However, in 2008 those pants were retired, which kind of makes you wonder: what do pants do when they retire? Surely there must be more to retirement than sitting in a museum display.

pants on safari   pants playing golf   pants gardening

FIVE-DOLLAR FARFALLE

2 x 2 inch ravioli stamp. **Pinch the center of the square** until it looks like a bowtie.

Repeat this process of rolling, cutting, and pinching until you have a satisfying amount farfalle for your dish. Once you have enough, **lay them all on a non-stick baking sheet**, spacing each one out so they aren't touching each other. Then **bake them** in a pre-heated oven at 350° for about five minutes — just enough time for them to develop a slight crust — so they don't clump together when you toss them with sauce.

For the sauce, we'll make a tomato vinaigrette. First, **dice the peppers, onions, olives, and half of the tomatoes** and **toss them into a mixing bowl with the red wine vinegar**. Take the other half of the tomatoes and **purée**

FAST FOOD FOR THOUGHT

The 16th-century inventor of farfalle — more commonly known as "bowtie pasta" — must have also invented time travel too because bowties hadn't been invented until 200 years later.

---

them in the food processor. Add that to a mixing bowl. **Dice up some chicken** and add it as well. **Mix the sauce** well and then **toss in the faux farfalle**.

Once all the bowties are coated, simply serve the pasta in a fancy bowl. *Presto!* The ladies will love this one!

128 FANCY PASTA & NOODLES

CHICKEN CHIPOTLIOLI

✳ ✳ ✳ ✳ ✳

Made with artistic integrity.

With all the pressure and persuasion these days to "go green," even fast food restaurants are jumping on the food bandwagon of social responsibility. One of the chains leading the charge is Chipotle Mexican Grill, which was actually once a part of the McDonald's corporate family for seven years, until Ronald McDonald and Chipotle founder Steve Ells split up because of, as they say in show business, "creative differences." You'd probably leave too if they made you wear an ensemble you didn't want to wear; Ells must have *hated* being in that Grimace costume all that time.

Mr. Ells went his own way — sans grimaces — to continue his Chipotle operation with a self-proclaimed "F.W.I. (Food With Integrity)" philosophy, which drives his company to buy local and organic vegetables when they can, and to buy meat from farms where animals are naturally raised. That's right, the carnitas in that taco once frolicked in the mud, and the barbacoa in that burrito once grazed in a grass field fertilized by its own manure — but at least that's nature's way.

However, no matter how much effort Chipotle puts in behind the scenes to strive for sustainable ingredients, the end result still looks like plain ol' fast food in a wrapper and a recyclable paper bag. This is where this your Fancy Fast Food cookbook comes in handy...

Ingredients (from Chipotle Mexican Grill):

1 Burrito with grilled chicken (or any meat of your preference), fresh tomato salsa, cheese, and lettuce (no rice and beans)
1 condiment cup of Tomatillo-red Chili Salsa

PLUS: organic basil leaves (for garnish and an extra touch of irony)

> **TIPS FROM AN EMPTY JAR**
>
> *When dealing with ingredients that are minimally-processed, rest assured that you can further process them quickly at the touch of a button with your food processor.*

First, **unwrap the burrito** and **separate the ingredients**: the tomatoes, cheese, lettuce, and grilled chicken. Put the chicken in a food processor and **grind it down** to a paste-like substance that we'll stuff inside the raviolis. We'll need to make the raviolis by hand, so **rinse off the empty tortilla**, which will serve as our sheet of "pasta" to cut them from.

To make one ravioli, first use a ravioli stamp to **cut out a serrated square** from the tortilla. (This will serve as the "top" of it. Before cutting out the bottom square, **spoon out a small amount of meat filling** and **place it on the area to be punched out. Place the first square inside the stamp**, so that when you cut through the bottom square, the filling is sandwiched in between to layers of tortilla. **Pinch the edges of the ravioli closed** with your fingers to seal in the meat. (The tortilla should still be moist enough from the rinsing that it should fuse easily.) **Repeat this ravioli-making process** until you have enough, or until you run out of tortilla, whichever comes first.

To make the sauce, **chop the tomatoes** down to a pulp and then **add it to the tomatillo-red chili salsa** and mix well. While you're at the cutting board, **finely chop the lettuce** to use as a garnish.

Finally, plate your meal: **place the raviolis on a nice-looking plate**, then **top it with the sauce, the chopped lettuce, and some cheese. Garnish it** with ironic basil and *voilà!* It's F.F.W.F. (Fast Food With Fanciness)!

ON FECAL MATTERS

Some places like Chipotle opt to get their meat from smaller farms instead from mega-meat facilities, not just because they claim to care about cows and pigs before they are brought to the slaughter, but because they prefer a meat production environment where meat isn't churned out on big assembly lines like Chevy Malibus. As anyone who's read or seen *Fast Food Nation* knows, this kind of factory environment is a nonstop operation, where standards can sometimes be overlooked because it goes too fast. It's sort of like that classic episode of *I Love Lucy* where Lucy and Ethel can't keep up with the candy coming down the conveyor belt — except instead of hiding chocolate in their mouths and blouses, the contents of an animal's digest tract (a.k.a. feces) sometimes hides in the meat and contaminates it with E. Coli. Sneaky feces! In other words, when it comes to mass-scale meat production, hey, sometimes shit really does happen.

CHEAT POTATO GNOCCHI

✳ ✳ ✳ ✳ ✳

One potato, two potato, sweet potato, more.

The Pacific Northwest is a region known for its beautiful landscape — majestic mountains, flowing rivers, dramatic coastlines, and lush, green woodlands — all of which might be completely awe-inspiring if not for the gloomy, consistent drizzle during eight months of the year. But that doesn't stop Pacific Northwesties from living life; they are a resilient and progressive bunch with a laid-back attitude and an affinity for the outdoors. (Hey, that's what rain jackets are for.) And while they are running, biking, or playing Frisbee golf outside, they are growing vegetables on farms and in hippie communes so that local, sustainable produce can be fed to the masses — even at the regional fast food chain Burgerville, which prides itself on a commitment to local businesses, farms and producers, thus reducing the carbon footprint.

Inspired by Pacific Northwesties, I journeyed to Oregon to conjure up a recipe — a *vegetarian* recipe no less — using Burgerville's popular sweet potato fries. My goal was to appease any of the environmentally conscious vegetarian fast foodies out there with at least one recipe — only to realize after the fact that, due to the time constraints of my visit there, I only had time to pick up the locally grown fries on the way to the airport and fly them over 2,400 miles back to the east coast, where I prepared them in my own kitchen. (Shame on me.)

Ingredients (from Burgerville):

1 Hamburger (or any burger; we just need the bun)
1 large order of Sweet Potato Fries
1 Side Salad
1 bottle of local water
1 soft drink of your choice

PLUS: organic parsley (for garnish and a touch of irony)

IMPORTING FAST FOOD

If you're not too concerned about the size of your carbon footprint, go ahead and fly fast food from other regions to your own kitchen yourself. With meals hardly being served on domestic American flights these days, airlines don't seem to mind if you bring bags of fast food in addition to your carry-ons. Generally, fast food will survive a five-hour journey — they're not delicate like soufflés or anything — provided you can resist from eating it, with the enticing smell circulating throughout the cabin (much to your fellow passengers' chagrin).

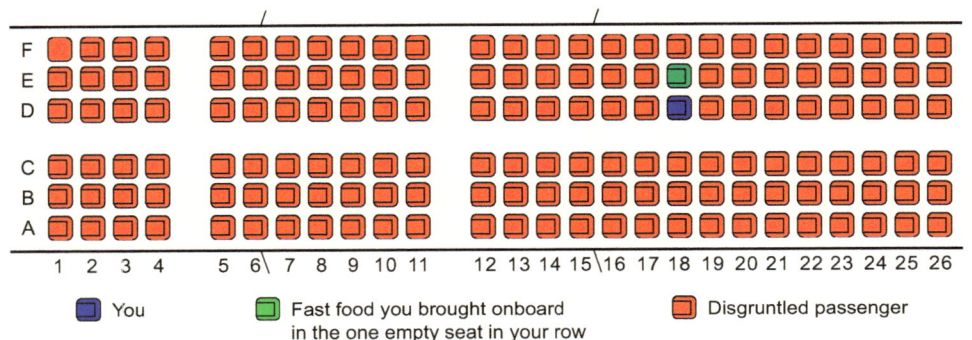

First, **break apart pieces of the burger bun** and **put it in a food processor with about 3 tablespoons of water** to make it soggy. **Add the cheese** from the side salad and **all of the sweet potato fries**. Then **blend it** until it becomes a bowl of sweet potato dough.

Knead the dough, then **roll pieces into small balls about ¾ inch in diameter**. Then slightly **squish each one down into an egg shape** with a fork, leaving a nice texture behind.

The gnocchi will fall apart if we boil them, so we're just going to leave them as is on a plate. **Finely chop some greens** from the salad and **sprinkle them over** as a garnish. **Top it off with ironic parsley** and serve with the soft drink in a nice glass. *Tada!* You can try this recipe with sweet potato fries from anywhere, whether you fly them across the country or not!

— FAST FOOD FOR THOUGHT —

The "g" in "gnocchi" has the right to remain silent. Anything it says can and will be used against it in a court of law.

134 Fancy Pasta & Noodles

HOW TO NICELY TELL A CARNIVORE TO EAT HIS DAMN VEGETABLES

Yes, there have been a lot of jokes about vegetarians in this book so far, but to be fair, it's an eating lifestyle that's completely fine, especially if you want your poop to look like algae. But I kid. Sure, there are many reasons why a vegetarian lifestyle is beneficial; countless studies have shown that an all-vegetable diet significantly reduces risks for illnesses such as coronary heart disease, diabetes, and kidney stones — and do you really want to go through the agony of passing one of those? From what I've heard, it's going to do *way* more than just tickle a little.

Additionally, a vegetarian lifestyle is not only good for you, it's good for the environment; meat production produces more waste and utilizes way more fossil fuels than vegetable production, which mostly just uses the power of the sun — and that's not going to burn out for another five billion years (or until Stephen Hawking's robot voice says so). So if you're a vegetarian trying to convince your meat-loving friends to switch sides, here are a few things you can say to try and win them over*:

- "Vegetarian food doesn't have to be bland; even four-year-olds can figure out that the same spices you use to season meat with, you could still use on vegetables — and they don't even know how to tie their own shoes yet."

- "Cows are natural herbivores, so why not cut out the middle man? It's like getting nutritional value at wholesale prices, without all that bloody overhead."

- "Um, have you seen Popeye's arms? If you lived on a diet of spinach, you might have to give away two tickets to the gun show too."

- "If you plant an apple the ground, you'll have a sustainable source of apples for years to come. If you plant a chicken wing in the ground, you'll have, well, a chicken wing in the ground."

- "Even Samuel L. Jackson, who once played Shaft, is a vegetarian — and he's one bad mother– *shut your mouth*."

* There's no guarantee you're going to change their minds. In the USA, they've got you outnumbered about 40 to 1.

This is why Santa's fat.

FANCY HOLIDAY MEALS

✻ ✻ ✻ ✻ ✻

Ah, the holidays... those times of the year when you express your love and support of age-old traditions with joy, good tidings, and gifts — gifts like unflattering horizontal-striped shirts that should definitely come with gift receipts. Let's face it, any clothes you give during the holidays — may they be flattering or not — should come with a return policy because they might not fit after all the festive eating and belt-loosening going on. But hey, it's the thought that counts, right?

Where I'm from, holidays are all about *food*, more than cards, gifts, dreidels, and whatever toys kids play with on Kwanzaa. Our red-letter days give us excuses to get together with loved ones to eat, drink, and be merry — whether we care for those loved ones or not — and what's not to like about a reason for a *feast*? Holiday meals are annual reminders that food is not just a means of sustenance, it's a transcendent phenomenon that has brought us together for millennia, no matter what our individual notions are about love, religion, or cheesy Hallmark cards. And the relationship between food and tradition will only continue on in the decades to come, as long as holidays are celebrated, the Food Network exists, and foodies perform the ritual of waiting in line for up to an hour to savor the latest offerings Tweeted about from a gourmet food truck. So loosen that belt, eat up, and enjoy your culinary traditions — just make sure you gargle before stepping up to the mistletoe.

A VALENTINE'S PAELLA YOSHINOLLA

✻ ✻ ✻ ✻ ✻

Nothing says Happy Valentine's Day to your sweetheart than heartburn.

This Valentine's Day treat that special someone to a romantic-looking dinner inspired by Spain — the passionate and amorous country that brought us the sensuous dance of flamenco and the aphrodisiacal delicacy of paella. But we're not going to break the budget at a fancy Spanish *taverna*; we're going to get our ingredients from The Original Beef Bowl fast food joint Yoshinoya — the perfect place to go for this mock paella recipe, not only because they have rice, but because they can also spice up your gastronomic love life with a little *shichimi-togarashi* (Japanese seven-spice chili powder). With this spicy recipe, you'll impress that special someone with your culinary passion — so don't forget to wear that "Kiss the Cook" apron! Just remember that when you make this, you might inadvertently be giving your special Valentine an added gift: acid reflux.

Ingredients for a questionably romantic dinner for two (from Yoshinoya):

1 Beef Short Rib and Chicken Plate
1 Grilled Shrimp Bowl
1 Miso Soup
1 Chicken Vegetable Soup
1 side order of Steamed Vegetables
2 condiment cups of *Shichimi-Togarashi* (seven spice chili powder)
2 condiment cups of *Beni Shoga* (pickled ginger)
2 soft drinks of your choice

First, **take all the rice** from your bowls and plates and **spread it evenly** at the base of a skillet. **Add the broth** from the soups and **simmer** over a low heat. Then **collect all the vegetables** from the bowls and plates and add those to the mixture as well. **Let it stew** for about 10 minutes.

Since we don't have the traditional coloring spice of saffron, we are going to spice things up with the colorful Japanese chili powder. **Distribute the shichimi-togarashi** generously in the skillet so that it infuses with all the rice and broth, and **stir**.

In this "yoshinolla" variation of paella, we're going to **add chicken, shrimp, and chorizo**. We don't actually have Spanish sausage, so we'll have to improvise and **cut the beef short ribs** into sliced sausage shapes. **Slice the chicken** while you're at it, and **butterfly the shrimp**.

Transfer the rice to a proper paella pan and **garnish the top** with your three meats, as well as some strips of pickled ginger for an additional splash of color. Pour your beverages in fancy wine glasses and — *tada!* — a romantic-looking dinner for you and your Valentine. Hope you told Cupid to pack the Tums.

TIPS FROM AN EMPTY JAR

It should go without say that this is probably not going to be the best tasting "paella" you've had, since you faked it — and faking it in the kitchen might lead to faking it in another room in the house (the one with the bed) — so as an insurance, it's probably best to have some backup reservations somewhere.

SLIDE RIGHT INTO MY HEART

Don't have access to a Yoshinoya Beef Bowl on Valentine's Day? Well you don't have to settle for a day of price-hiked bouquets and generic heart-shaped boxes of bon-bons; you can take that special someone to your local White Castle for their annual Valentine's Date Night — just be sure to make reservations. They will provide a "romantic" atmosphere, complete with decorations, tablecloths, candles, a special Valentine's Day menu, and waiter service. Not only will they satisfy your love of kitsch, but your craving for their signature White Castle sliders — those little steamed beef burgers that will go straight to your heart (in more ways than one). And if your Valentine is completely enamored by your choice in fine dining, who knows what it may lead to? White Castle has hosted white, arguably trashy, fairy-tale weddings — it is a *castle* after all.

140   Fancy Holiday Meals

FRANKSGIVING DINNER

✶ ✶ ✶ ✶ ✶

This Turkey Day, give franks.

Ah, Thanksgiving, that wholesome American holiday that celebrates the first harvest produced by the first European settlers with the help of the indigenous people. Today, the holiday often skips over the part in American history when the European settlers killed off the indigenous people — almost to the point of extinction — and goes right to the part when big inflated balloons parade down New York City's Broadway and the remaining indigenous people run casinos.

The concept of a traditional Thanksgiving dinner hasn't changed much over the decades; it's a gathering of family and friends over a big turkey — the centerpiece of the meal — a great bounty of poultry, especially when you get it free by collecting enough supermarket rewards points like my parents do. Each fourth Thursday of November, the ritual goes on in millions of American households: someone carves the bird, someone opens a can of jiggly cranberry sauce, and in the end, everyone eats and gets really drowsy from the all sleep-inducing tryptophan found in turkey meat — which really does put a damper on any post-dinner activity. So here's an alternative dinner you can prepare without turkey or the hours of prep, so you might stay awake for that 24-hour marathon of your favorite old television shows and movies.

Ingredients to serve a family of four (from Nathan's):

4 Nathan's World Famous Hot Dogs (with chili)
4 Corn Dogs on a Stick
4 orders of Crinkle-Cut French fries
4 small Fruit Punches

PLUS: organic chives (for garnish and an extra touch of irony)

To get started, use a kitchen torch to **sear one side of each of the corn dogs** so that they have a few burn marks — but not too much; just enough to give the exteriors an appearance of being roasted. Then flip each corn dog over and **cut an incision** so that you can **extract about two-thirds of each of the hot dogs** within. With those solid masses removed, you can easily **mold the corn bread batter** of the partially hollowed out corn dogs into shapes that resemble that of turkey legs.

Next, **remove the hot dogs from their buns**, leaving the chili. **Scoop the chili into a skillet**, and then **chop the remaining buns into small pieces. Mix two-thirds of the bun pieces** in with the chili — **crushing the beans** in the process — until they're blended and look like stuffing. To make the mashed potatoes, **put all the fries in a food processor** and **blend**. (The insides of Nathan's fries are usually already moist, so there's no need to add water.)

To make some faux cranberry sauce, **bring the fruit punch to a boil** in a nonstick pan until it's reduced down to a thick, red syrup. **Toss in the remaining bread pieces** to soak up the syrup and make a chunky paste with fruity flavor.

Finally, the plating: place your corn dog "turkey legs" and all the sides onto welcoming place settings for four. **Garnish the potatoes** with ironic chives. Now give thanks that you'll stay awake, and have a Happy Franksgiving!

FAST FOOD FOR THOUGHT

At the first Thanksgiving, the European settlers failed to realize that the Native Americans might actually not be "Indians," even though there wasn't any curry, paneer, or basmati rice at the table.

SWEET DREAMS ARE MADE OF THESE

Since you don't have all that tryptophan-laced turkey in you, here are some other ways to make you sleepy:

- Tune into a congressional hearing on C-SPAN.
- Drink milk that has been heated to the point that it develops that weird film on top of the saucepan.
- Take a long drive at night on a monotonous interstate highway for hours. (Warning: sleep may be disrupted when colliding into deer or eighteen-wheelers.)
- If you went to your parents' house for Franksgiving dinner, have your mom secretly slip you some roofies.
- Drink a bottle of tequila. (Side effects may include slurred speech, obnoxiousness, table dancing, bar fights, embarrassing phone calls to ex-significant others, and/or stupid-looking tattoos you'll regret the next morning.)
- Rub one out, flog the dolphin, wax the carrot, beat the meat, choke the chicken, slap the salami, drain the vein, spank the monkey, yank your crank*, or alternatively, simply have sex with an actual person.
- Have a nightcap cocktail of club soda and Robitussin.
- Give into traditional conformity, and just go out and eat a turkey sandwich — or pop an Ambien.

* Oh, the list goes on and on...

BUBBE WENDY'S HANUKKAH LATKES

* * * * *

Dry and ready.

Hey everybody, it's Hanukkah! It's Chanuka! No matter how you spell it, it's time for the Jewish festival of lights — eight crazy nights of dreidels gone wild, a time when the gelt is as abundant as the guilt from old yentas around a table playing canasta. But you don't need to be Jewish to partake in Hanukkah traditions, particularly the culinary treat of latkes. "Latkes" is Yiddish for fried pancakes, typically of the potato variety — making them oddly similar to McDonald's hash browns. However, Bubbe Wendy has guilted me into using her Fancy Fast Food recipe — "If you just want to use McDonald's hash browns, then I guess that's fine by me..." — so here goes. *Oy vey...*

Ingredients for a small Hanukkah party (from Wendy's):

8 orders of Hash Browns (for the eight nights of Hanukkah)
2 Baked Potatoes (with packets of sour cream and Buttery-Best Spread)
2 packs of Apple Slices
1 small soft drink
1 bottle of water
packets of Sweet & Sour sauce
packets of salt and pepper

PLUS: organic chives (for garnish and a touch of irony); and a pinch of Jewish guilt (may be substituted with reduced-fat Catholic guilt)

— TIPS FROM AN EMPTY JAR —

When arguing with Bubbe Wendy that the latkes do in fact resemble McDonald's hash browns like you told her, let her win the argument — she's been through a lot and could use the validation. In the end, she'll still try and make you feel guilty for never calling her anyway.

First, take all the mini hash brown nuggets and **mush them in a mixing bowl** with your hands. Touching them, you'll realize they are all too greasy to stick together, so we'll need to make a batter to work as a binding agent. **Skin one of the baked potatoes**, and put it into a food processor with a little bit of water. **Add the resulting potato batter** to the bowl of mushed hash browns and **mix thoroughly**. **Add salt and pepper** as desired.

In a large skillet, **melt a few packets of Bubbe Wendy's "Buttery-Best Spread"**; there's enough oil in it for a fry-up. While it melts, **slice the top of your beverage's paper cup** so you can use the resulting ring as a guide when you **pour the potato batter in the skillet. Fry each latke** on both sides until it becomes crispy and golden brown.

Latkes are traditionally served with apple sauce or sour cream. We already have the latter, so we're going to have to make the apple sauce. Simply **take all the apple slices** and **purée them** in a blender with a half teaspoon of Sweet & Sour sauce and a little bit of water. Be careful not to add too much water or it will turn into apple juice.

Finally the plating: **place all the latkes on a fancy serving platter**, and **garnish them** with ironic chives. **Serve them with the makeshift apple sauce, and the sour cream** that came with the baked potatoes. Now light that menorah, spin those dreidels, and have a Happy Hanukkah!

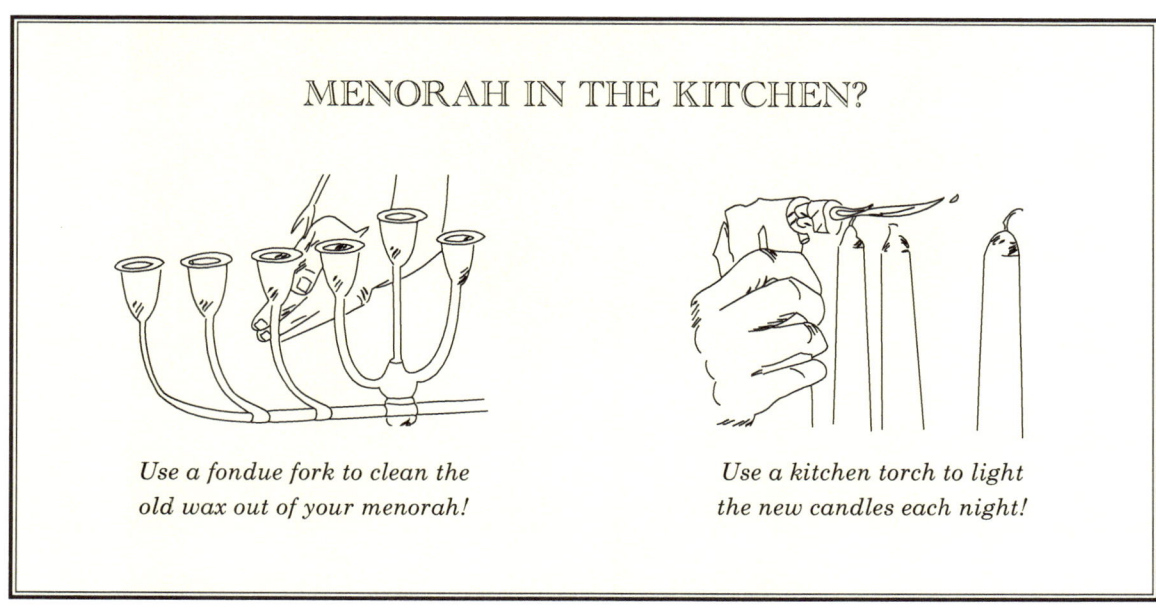

MENORAH IN THE KITCHEN?

Use a fondue fork to clean the old wax out of your menorah!

Use a kitchen torch to light the new candles each night!

BUBBE WENDY'S HANUKKAH LATKES

HONEY APPLE GLAZED CHRISTMAS HOLIDAY HAM

✳ ✳ ✳ ✳ ✳

Slightly better than a lump of coal.

'Twas the night before Christmas, and all through the house, not a creature was stirring… except for you, the Fancy Fast Food Chef, stirring apple filling and honey mustard in a saucepan for a makeshift version of a traditional Christmas dish!

Of course, we are talking about the traditional holiday ham, the centerpiece at many a Christmas dinner. Unfortunately, a whole cured hind leg of a pig is something that fast food restaurants will probably never sell — even if you wish for it while sitting on Santa's lap at the mall — so we'll have to use our creative muscle, tweak a little language, and perform a Christmas miracle with *ham*-burgers instead. But first let's make a list and check it twice, and find out which ingredients are naughty or nice*:

Ingredients for a family of five people who will still be hungry afterwards, since they probably won't eat this (from Burger King):

8 BK Quad Stackers
3 Double Croissan'wiches (each with double ham and no cheese)
1 BK Kids Meal (with Burger Shots and a toy)
3 Dutch Apple Pies
3 juiceboxes of Apple Juice
1 Garden Salad (with honey mustard dressing)

* *They're all naughty.*

148 Fancy Holiday Meals

FAST FOOD FOR THOUGHT

With your purchase of eight BK Quad Stackers, do the math: 8 x 4 = 32 patties! That's enough to stack them in one pile and play a pretty meaty game of Jenga.

Cut each of the 32 beef patties into smaller pieces so that they fit in a food processor — not all at once, of course. As much as your appliance can handle at a time, **grind the beef chunks with the bacon and cheese. Repeat this process** until all the meat is ground up.

Mold the ground beef into the shape of a ham. Then, **score the back of the "ham"** in a diagonal grid — like one might do on the real thing. To continue the façade, **sear the outside with a kitchen torch**.

What you have now almost looks like a ham, but it won't slice like one — this is where breakfast comes in. **Take all the ham out of the Croissan'wiches** and **drape a couple of slices over the side** of your wad of meat so it looks

HONEY APPLE GLAZED CHRISTMAS HOLIDAY HAM   149

FAST FOOD FOR THOUGHT

The 32-patty wad of meat is pliable enough to be molded into anything Christmas-related, whether it be a figure of Baby Jesus, one of the three kings, or simply a snowman —you can pretend that he is Parson Brown!

---

like there's actually ham inside. **Use toothpicks** to keep the real ham slices from falling, then **pinch the edges** so the meat wad and slices look seamless. **Pile additional slices of ham** in front of the mold to pretend that it was all carved from the same place.

The final touch is the glaze. **Bring all the apple juice to a boil** in a nonstick skillet so that it starts reducing. **Add in the apple filling** from the pies, and then the **packet of honey mustard** from the salad. Once it's all blended together, **brush the glaze** over your counterfeit ham with a pastry brush.

Finally, the plating: **place your ham-like creation on top of a bed of lettuce** on a fancy white platter. **Garnish the sides** with tomatoes, carrots, and more honey apple glaze. Now look at it with awe; it's a Christmas miracle!

To go a step even further, take your kids meal toy and make it into an ornament. Roll a straw wrapper into string and loop it around the doll. Looks great on a tree!

150 Fancy Holiday Meals

FONDUE DU SEPT-ONZE

✳ ✳ ✳ ✳ ✳

Drop the ball on your New Year's diet with this one.

One of the most common New Year's resolutions that people make each year is to go on a diet. While this resolution is easy to make, it's hard to keep, for many people slip back into their old eating habits in merely a couple of weeks, just in time for Martin Luther King Jr. Day — a national holiday when we can truly honor Dr. King's famous "I Have A Dream" speech by stuffing our faces with black-and-white cookies.

Here's a dream for you: what if we could eat whatever we wanted, whenever we wanted without consequences, feeling bloated, or special surgery? We could eat as much cheese, barbecue, steaks, or greasy junk food as we wanted, and win a bunch of T-shirts in *Man Vs. Food*-like eating challenges in the process! Of course this is a pipe dream, and so we're just going to have to stick to making that resolution to diet each New Year's — but not without one last indulgent hurrah before the stroke of midnight.

Here's an indulgent Fancy Fast Food recipe you can make when all other meal plans have fallen through on December 31st, and every place has closed early except for 7-Eleven. While you could get some regular groceries there, let's play by the rules and only stock up on their classic, branded fast food items by the register and automated hot dog roller.

Ingredients for a small party (from 7-Eleven):

1 pack of 7-Eleven White Corn Nachos with melted cheese (make sure you pour as much cheese as you can on the *bottom* of the plastic container)
2 7-Eleven ¼-Pound Big Bite Hot Dogs
1 Big Gulp with ¾ 7-Up, ¼ Coca-Cola (mix it up so it looks like Champagne)
1 bottle of 7-Select Spring Water

FAST FOOD FOR THOUGHT

Many people make the resolution to diet because most of us seem to put on some added weight each year, often so subtly that we don't realize it until 10 years later while looking at pictures of our younger selves and say, "Wow, look how much thinner I used to be."

Remove the nacho chips from the plastic container to separate the chips and cheese. Then, carefully **pour out the cheese** into a ceramic fondue caquelon. **Set the caquelon over a flame** and **stir in half a cup of water** to thin out the mixture. **Let it simmer**.

Next, **place the nacho chips in a steamer** to soften them up. While that's going, **slice the two hot dogs** two ways: one should be bias-cut diagonally into long slices; the other should be cut into small 3-inch strips. Take each strip and **wrap a softened nacho chip around it**, and **fasten it with a toothpick**. Place your "sausage" hors d'oeuvres on a fancy white plate.

Cut the hot dog buns into bite-sized squares, and **place them in a fancy bowl. Pour the soft drink mixture into wine glasses** and serve them alongside the sausage, bread bowl, and fondue pot. Now get out your noisemakers and get ready! *Ten… Nine… Eight… Seven… Eleven…!*

DID SOMEBODY SAY CHEESE?

We cannot talk about a *faux fondue du fromage* without paying tribute to one of the greatest foods ever invented: cheese. Nothing quite creates a harmony of texture, taste, and euphoria the way cheese does so perfectly in its each of its hundreds of varieties. Cheese not only melts in our mouths and prompts us to smile, but it thankfully also gives us a scapegoat to point our fingers to when we "cut" it. There are so many types of cheese out there — too many to mention in a single page — but here are some of the more popular ones in the realm of fast food:

Type	Usages	Why It's Awesome
Cheddar	tacos, cheesesteaks, macaroni and cheese	This well-dressed cheese is so sharp — or even extra sharp — that it's become a colloquialism for riches in rap songs, yo.
Mozzarella	pizza, fried cheese sticks	Without this cheese, a regular slice of pizza just looks like a big tomato sauce stain that just *won't* come out on an infomercial, no matter how much of that other brand you use.
Swiss	bacon Swiss mushroom burgers, fried chicken sandwiches	This holey and celestial cheese really knows how to melt and drape itself beautifully on the side of a burger, and on the surface of the moon in children's books.
American	grilled cheese sandwiches, classic cheeseburgers	When cheese (or politics) is involved, nothing says American quite like something with a lot of process involved — but it's also the ideal cheese for a melting pot.
Blue	buffalo wings, celery	When made into a dressing, it's so tangy and delicious that wings and celery seem to exist solely as a conduit for getting it from the cup to your mouth — because drinking it straight like a shot is just plain gross.

There's always room for dessert.

FANCY DESSERTS

* * * * *

Remember when you were a kid at dinner and you begged to eat your dessert first? While some parents obliged, many didn't permit such an act for they were trying to teach you the true order of the world: that desserts are the reward at the *end* of a meal when you've finished eating all your damn vegetables. Little did your anagram-incapable young mind know that when it comes to desserts, doing things backwards sometimes makes grown-ups "stressed."

By design, dessert is the last, but certainly not least, part of a multi-course meal. It is meant to restore balance in our mouths from typically savory dishes and seal our taste buds with a sweet kiss. In layman's terms, dessert is the little red caboose at the end of the meal train for when you want to chew-chew one last time before the meal train go bye-bye. No matter how full we may feel after gorging on an entrée, there's somehow always room for dessert; desserts perpetually find a way to seduce us, indulge us, and make us feel naughty. Since we're already being naughty playing with fast food, we might as well have our cake and eat it too, by transforming it into something fancy, something no kid — or adult — can resist.

BOSTON KRÈME BRÛLÉE & FRUIT TART

✻ ✻ ✻ ✻ ✻

If you play with fire, you'll get burned.

I'm guessing that whoever invented *crème brûlée* loved two things, the first one being cream. And what lactose-tolerant person doesn't love cream? It's so rich and indulgent that it can metaphysically refer to itself in the superlative phrase, *"crème de la crème."* And when you mix cream with some sugar and vanilla and freeze it, you have a tasty frozen dessert that's so chic, it ameliorates any slice of pie with the sophisticated label, *"à la mode."**

The other thing the inventor of crème brûlée must have loved is playing with fire. What pyromaniac chef doesn't like to play with fire? Here's a fun, fire-blazing recipe that will combine the two joys, and hopefully not involve setting off the smoke detectors or calling the fire department. But first, it's time to buy the donuts…

**Ingredients
(from Dunkin' Donuts):**

8 Boston Kreme Donuts
3 Strawberry-Filled Donuts
1 Vanilla Kreme Donut
1 Cappuccino
1 bottle of water
packets of sugar

PLUS: organic mint leaves
(for garnish and an added touch of irony)

* *That's French for "to the mode," which really makes no sense when you take it out of context.*

156 FANCY DESSERTS

First, use a bread knife to **cut open each of the dozen donuts** to expose its filling. **Scoop out all of the custard filling** from the Boston Kreme donuts into a small ramekin. Then, **even off the top with a knife** or spatula and **let it chill** in the refrigerator for half an hour.

In the meantime, we'll make a fruit tart with the leftover donut shells. To make a small 4-inch one, **place 5–6 donut halves into a food processor** and **add about 3 tablespoons of the bottled water. Blend it down** until it becomes dough, then **mold it** into a 4-inch mini tart or quiche pan. **Bake it** in a preheated oven for 10–15 minutes at 400° F.

After it cools down to room temperature, **scoop out all the strawberry filling** from the strawberry-filled donuts onto the tart crust. **Top it off with a dollop of vanilla cream** from inside the Vanilla Kreme donut.

When the ramekin of custard is chilled, **sprinkle a layer of sugar** on top. Then **caramelize the sugar with a kitchen torch** until it develops a brown shell. **Garnish it** with ironic mint leaves and *voilà!* With the fancy fruit tart and the cappuccino served in a fancy cup, now America runs on crème brûlée!

TIPS FROM AN EMPTY JAR

I've added recipe instructions here for a fruit tart so that the eight de-creamed donuts don't go to waste. Of course, you could always just eat them without the cream, give them to a food shelter, or bring them to the office and leave them in the break room as a prank on April Fool's Day.

BOSTON KRÈME BRÛLÉE & FRUIT TART

CULVOUTIS

✿ ✿ ✿ ✿ ✿

The recipe name that sounds like a venereal disease.

Unless you're a complete virgin to French desserts, you know that a *clafoutis* is a fruit tart of buttery batter, traditionally made with cherries. Clafoutis originated from the cherry-pickin' province of Limousin in central France, which is an administrative territory whose name was unofficially licensed to American prom committees when they were trying to figure out a name for those really long cars that took high school seniors out to the big school dance. ("Extend-O-Car" didn't quite sound classy enough.) Coincidentally, it has been prom night that, according to tradition, usually ends up involving another activity involving cherries — "cherry-*popping*" — if you're lucky, that is.

Virgin or not, you can still enjoy popping cherries (into your mouth) as you prepare this recipe that will make anyone yearning for more. Better bring some protection.

Ingredients (from Culver's):

4 ButterBurgers
1 Custard Sundae with cherry topping
2 extra servings of cherry topping
1 cup of water

158 Fancy Desserts

Pick the cherries off the custard and **slice them into halves**. Do the same with the extra cherries you asked nicely for. Then **rinse them** all off in a colander.

For the buttered batter, take the buns of the *Butter*Burgers, **tear them** into smaller pieces, and **put them in a food processor. Add about 3 tablespoons of water** and **mix it down** until it becomes a dough. **Fill a small ramekin** with that dough, and **top it with cherry halves**.

Bake the clafoutis in a preheated oven for about 20 minutes at 400°F. Then **let it cool** before serving. If this is your first *faux* clafoutis, it's okay if you mess up; no one ever gets it right the first time.

PICKING FRUITS AND VEGETABLES

Most of the fruits and vegetables called for in the recipes of this satirical cookbook were most likely grown on factory farms, picked by low-paid farm hands of commercially minded farmers, washed by machines, sold to distributors, driven miles across America in trucks, handled by low-wage employees, and delivered straight to you, in plastic containers or inside greasy sandwiches. How's that for "fresh?" The only way they could be fresher is if they were to be given to you in slow-motion, with attractive drops and splashes of clear water flying everywhere (like in TV commercials).

Unless you're one of those devoutly anti-veggie carnivores who laughs at the thought of even touching a vegetable — you know who you are — you may find yourself picking fresh vegetables from a place that doesn't smother them in fatty dressings or chili made from yesterday's old hamburgers. Here's a quick guide on picking some of the produce that you might otherwise just get in a burger, salad shaker, or dessert:

Lettuce: Pull off a full leaf from the head. If you can fan it towards your face and feel a little breeze, it's crisp enough.
Tomatoes: Be as selective as Goldilocks. If you sleep on a bed of tomatoes and you have back problems the next morning, they're too hard. If you lay down and immediately crush them, they're too soft. Firm mattresses made of tomatoes are just right.
Onions: If you're on Prozac and they still make you cry, you know they're fresh.
Apples: Check for wormholes; if you suddenly find yourself in another dimension of the space-time continuum, you probably shouldn't buy that one.
Cherries: If you're getting them fresh from a farmer, make sure his last name isn't Maraschino.

BLIZZARD BLINTZ

✤ ✤ ✤ ✤ ✤

Scoring touchdowns with grandmothers everywhere.

A blintz is a delicacy that originated from Russia and Eastern Europe, a recipe that came to America on an immigrant ship and landed at Ellis Island, where it was put into quarantine for a few days and had its name shortened from Blintzensteinski. Fortunately, the blintz made it into this country without much more of a hitch so that it could be passed on from generation to generation by grandmothers who reminisced about "the Old Country." Blintzes — the Yiddish term for thin pancakes similar to *crêpes* — may be served in many sweet or savory ways depending on what you fill them with, but one popular variation is packed with cheese, topped off with fruit, and served as a dessert.

Now that the blintz is in America, it should not be confused with the "blitz," the defensive play in American football where a linebacker bum-rushes and attempts to tackle the quarterback behind the line of scrimmage — although it would be pretty funny if you asked your grandmother for a blintz and, because of her loss of hearing, she came storming out of the kitchen yelling "AAAAAAAHHHH!!!" before tackling you on the dining room floor.

Ingredients (from Dairy Queen):

1 Strawberry CheeseQuake Blizzard
1 Sundae with cherry topping
4 Hamburgers
1 bottle of water

First, **put the Blizzard in the freezer**; it will need to be as frozen as possible if it's going to have some sort of consistency of cheese when it inevitably melts later. While you're at it, **put the sundae in too** so the cherry topping and ice cream remain separated.

Next, **take apart all the hamburgers**; you'll only need the buns for this dessert. **Break them into small pieces** and **put them in a food processor**. **Add 3 tablespoons of water**, and **blend**. Instead of a doughy, kneadable substance like in many other recipes found in this book, it should be more of a liquid, like pancake batter.

Heat up a nonstick skillet and **pour in the bun-based batter**. **Let the pancake brown** on one side before **flipping it over** to brown on the other side. When both sides have browned, **let it cool** to room temperature; the warmer it is, the faster the ice cream you will put inside will melt, which is something you don't want.

When its ready, **place the pancake on a plate**, then **scoop out some Blizzard** in the center to be the cheese filling — it's "CheeseQuake," after all. Then **roll it up** on both sides and **top it off with the sundae's cherry topping**. *Tada!* It's just like Grandma used to make, if she was ever locked in a Dairy Queen.

MAGGIE MOUSSE

✻ ✻ ✻ ✻ ✻

Stop the violence; eat more ice cream.

Here's an old children's riddle that I remember from elementary school: *Why is a chef mean? Because he beats the eggs and whips the cream.* While that may provide a chuckle for a third grader, the adulthood reality is that chefs really *can* be mean — hell, straight-out foul-mouthed assholes sometimes. I mean, have you seen Gordon Ramsay on *Hell's Kitchen?* That guy drops more than an angry F bomb between every other word whenever he's disparaging chefs and patrons with furious rants like:

- "I'd rather eat poodle [BLEEP] than put that in my mouth."
- "I'll get more pumpkin, and I'll ram it up your [BLEEPING] ass."
- "[BLEEP] off you fat useless sack of [BLEEPING] Yankee dandee doodle [BLEEP]."

It's actually a little dangerous watching the show on television because there's so much bleeping going on that it can be hard to tell whether or not your smoke detector is going off, alerting you of a fire.

But I digress. The beating of eggs and whipping of cream kind of makes you think of all the violent acts that go on during the cooking process. Think about it: a kitchen is a virtual arsenal of sharp knives, blunt weapons, and devices with the ability to burn things, and a chef is constantly beating, whipping, cutting, chopping, mashing, shredding, pounding, crushing, and putting things into oven death chambers. It's a miracle that more chefs haven't turned into serial killers or genocidal maniacs, but perhaps that's because they're taking out all their frustrations and psychotic episodes on meats and vegetables — or perhaps they're just saving their tantrums for camera in attempts for more entertaining television.

Here's a peaceful, nonviolent mock mousse recipe that doesn't involve the traditional and torturous methods of whipping cream and beating eggs. While it won't technically be a mousse, you'll have piece of mind knowing that no eggs or cartons of cream were harmed during the making of this recipe.

Ingredients (from Maggie Moo's):

1 medium cup of Dark Chocolate Ice Cream (ask them to put some nonviolent canned whipped cream around it)

1 hot fudge topping (on the side)

PLUS: organic mint leaves (for garnish and a touch of irony)

First, **scoop the whipped cream off** onto a separate plate and **put it in the refrigerator** before it melts. What's left is the chocolate ice cream, which will be transformed into the "mousse." You could let it melt for a bit, whisk it, and serve it in a fancy glass, but for this variation, we are going to put it in a mold. The medium paper cup you bought it in already should suffice, so just **pack it all down** with a spoon and spatula. Then put the mold in the freezer to let it harden. **Leave the hot fudge out** and bring it down to room temperature.

--- TIPS FROM AN EMPTY JAR ---

When freezing the ice cream mold, make sure your freezer is set to its coldest setting; we want it to become as stiff and hard as Guy Fieri's spiky hair.

--- FAST FOOD FOR THOUGHT ---

"I scream, you scream, we all scream for ice cream!" There's no substitute for the real thing — because nothing really rhymes with "yogurt" or "Tofutti."

After a few hours, take the mousse mold out of the freezer and **use a knife to cut through the paper cup** on one side and then **tear off the rest of the paper. Pop the bottom of the cup off**, and place the mold on a fancy white plate. You'll see that at room temperature, it will start to melt immediately, so be quick. **Use a knife to spread the fudge** on top of the mold, then **garnish it** with some ironic mint and a dollop of the saved whipped cream. Mousse is served!

MAGGIE MOUSSE

CONSPIRACY THEORIES IN THE DESSERT

Area 51 may be a secured warehouse in the Nevada desert housing all the supposed evidence of UFOs and other such conspiracy theories, but did you know there are conspiracies closer to home, involving the very desserts you might have eaten last night? Quick, someone call the *Weekly World News!*

- Did you ever wonder why it's called "carrot cake" when the generally sweet baked good tastes *nothing* like carrots? That's right, there's been a plot brewing since medieval times when vegetarian monks baked carrot cakes as ploy to get sinful carnivores to eat their damned vegetables by masking them with sugar, vanilla, and cinnamon. Their plan evidently worked; carrot cake has infiltrated many parts of the world in our modern age, along with the secretively sweet recipe for zucchini bread.

- Before Kraft Foods branded their gelatin dessert with the name "Jell-O" — which subsequently became used as the generic term for all gelatin products — the government used the acronym J.E.L.L.O. as a code name for a big, alien hyena-like creature: Jumbo Extraterrestrial Long Laughing Object. Not surprisingly, it didn't think its name was funny either.

- Forget what you may have heard about the origin of red velvet cake; its origin actually dates back to the 18th century in Transylvania, where it was baked by a secret sect of vampires who wanted to hide their thirst of human blood with baked goods. As the recipe was carried on through generations, they replaced the blood with beet juice, and eventually red food dye, and renamed it "red velvet cake" — not only to shroud their presence, but to create a diversion from the fact that their vampire robes were not actually velvet, but made out of an embarrassingly cheap polyester blend.

- In a very rare painting by Leonardo Da Vinci, Jesus Christ is depicted having the dessert course at the Last Supper with the Twelve Apostles. On his plate is a yellow cake given to him by the Angel Gabriel — angel food cake! This, of course, debunks Dan Brown's fictitious *Da Vinci Code* theory that the Holy Grail is the secret that Mary Magdalene is the wife of Christ, but that it's actually the *dessert* of Christ at the Last Supper — which means that the holy, modern-day descendant of the true Grail is quite possibly... a pack of Twinkies!

166   FANCY DESSERTS

TIRAMISU DI TIMIO

✳ ✳ ✳ ✳ ✳

Oh, Canada...

The border between the United States and Canada is the world's largest undefended border, spanning about 5,500 miles long. It remains unguarded because Canada, at least to the American majority, is no real threat — it's almost a counterpart of America anyway. It's been nicknamed "America's Little Brother," "America's Biggest Suburb," and "America's Frosted Hat" amongst other things, which might seem like fightin' words to any other country, but in this case the Canadians are just so nice. Have you heard this one? *What did the Canadian say when an American accidentally stepped on his foot? "Sorry, eh?"*

However, not all Canadians are that dry; amongst the contributions from our friendly, hockey-loving neighbors in The Great White North are comedic actors (i.e., Mike Myers), blonde bombshells (i.e., Pamela Anderson), and Tim Hortons, the Canadian coffee, sandwich, and donut chain, which has dozens of locations within our American borders. Many Americans don't know that Tim Hortons is actually named after the famous hockey player Tim Horton, a Canadian national legend who really has little to do with making sandwiches or coffee these days — nor anything to do with making Italian desserts derived from donuts for that matter. With that said, we're going to have to be proactive Americans and take that initiative, so that the Canadians can go about doing what they do best: asking for things politely.

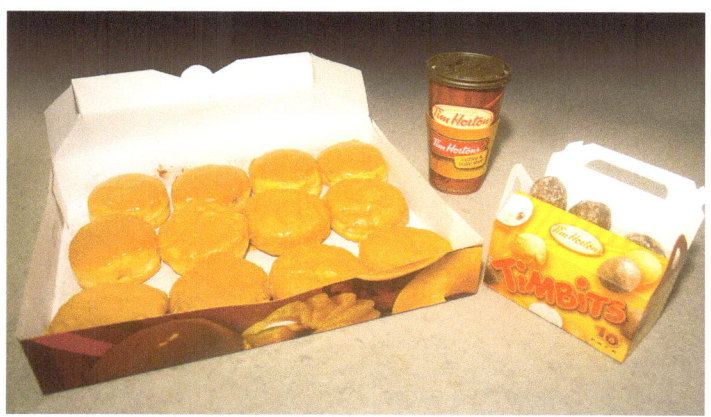

Ingredients (from Tim Hortons):

1 dozen Canadian Maple Donuts
1 small box of Chocolate-Glazed Timbits
1 large Coffee

First, **slice the Timbits** in halves and **place them flat side down** on a nonstick baking sheet. **Bake them** in a preheated oven at 400°F for about 15–20 minutes, and then **let them cool** so that they get hard and crumbly.

Meanwhile, **cut open the Canadian maple donuts**, and **extract their creamy fillings** into a bowl. You now have a pile of empty donut halves; cut them into rectangular "ladyfinger" shapes.

Pour some of the coffee into a bowl and then **dip each ladyfinger** in it; make it moist enough to mold, but not fall apart. With each moistened ladyfinger, **build a layer of cake** in a mini-bread pan. The next layer of the tiramisu is the cream, so **add a layer of that** on top of the ladyfingers, and then **flatten it down** before adding another layer of coffee-infused ladyfingers and one more layer of cream. When that's done, **let it chill** in the refrigerator for at least an hour.

Take the dessert out of the pan, **cut it into smaller servings**, and place each on a fancy white plate. Garnish the top by **grating the hardened chocolate-glazed Timbits** into a thin layer of powder, and serve with coffee. *Presto!* An Italian dessert inspired by a hockey player! *GOAL!*

FAST FOOD FOR THOUGHT

Here's some coffee talk: lady fingers — they contain no ladies nor fingers. Discuss.

PIN A LEAF ON IT

In diner jargon, "pin a rose on it," means "add onions." In Canada, pinning a leaf on it is when Canadians take familiar American logos and suddenly make them Canadian by putting a maple leaf on it:

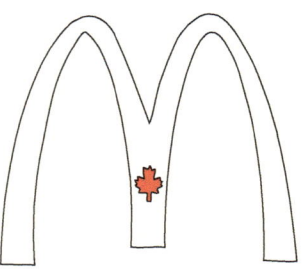 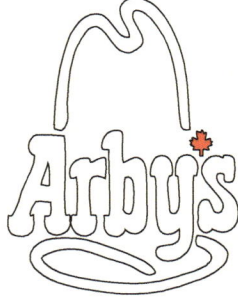 

FANCIFY YOUR COFFEE

Coffee is a whole other gastronomic art form, with so many different types of beans, grinds, roasts, and preparation techniques that coffee snobs have become a class all their own. While some view coffee merely as a means to stay awake for an all-night study session or to keep from falling asleep at their cubicle desks, others view it as a classy post-dinner stimulant to keep the conversation going — or simply to offset the impending food coma from a big meal. Then again, there are those people who drink decaffeinated coffee, which is about as silly as a nonalcoholic beer.

Did you know that your run-of-the-mill cup of joe can also be made elite, and without having to bring out the fancy china either? Here's how:

Step One:
Take the lid off of your ordinary generic coffee shop coffee. *(Warning: Contents may be extremely hot, so please don't sue me.)*

Step Two:
Find an empty Starbucks cup and pour your coffee into it. Make it sound elitist by calling it a *"grande."*

Step Three:
Place a lid on top of the cup. *PRESTO!* Now go sell this for 2–3 times the amount of what you paid!

*Yes, **you** can make fast food look this fancy.*

FANCY CONCLUSION

✽ ✽ ✽ ✽ ✽

Now that you've read every ironic Fancy Fast Food recipe (or at least skimmed through some of them), you're ready to create some of your own! Just remember a few key things that you've learned from this book:

- No matter how you fancy you prepare it, chicken tastes like… chicken.
- "Organic" becomes "ironic" when you put fresh, organic herb garnishes on top of processed foods.
- Kitchen torches aren't just for lighting cigars or birthday candles anymore.
- There are only two types of fish in the fast food sea: grilled and fried.
- Eating meat can be a completely enjoyable experience — except maybe when trying to eat a vegan.
- People will eat almost anything if you put it on a pot, add water, boil it up, and call it a soup.
- If you use your imagination and creativity, you can find "ham" in a "hamburger."
- Fast food may not seem so unhealthy if it doesn't look like it is!*

Now go get yourself some burgers, fries, pizzas, burritos, and other fast foods, bring them to your kitchen, and start getting fancy!

Submit your best Fancy Fast Food recipes and photos (before and after shots, plus some photos of the process) to *fancyfastfood@gmail.com*, and they could be showcased on FancyFastFood.com! (Just make sure you follow the rules: all ingredients must come from the same fast food chain restaurant, and you can't add anything else — except for an ironic piece of garnish, of course.)

---

* It's still most likely going to be loaded with fat and sodium, but that's okay; many real gourmet dishes are too.

BEHIND THE
FANCY FAST FOOD

❋ ❋ ❋ ❋ ❋

FANCY FAST FOOD STARTED OUT AS A WACKY FOOD BLOG that launched in May of 2009, one where the worlds of fast food and gourmet food porn came colliding together like frying oil and balsalmic in a weird, fat-ladened vinaigrette. I'm not really a chef — nor do I claim to be — I just play one on the Internet. I don't have any formal training in the culinary arts at all, except for this one "knife skills" class I took when I started to occasionally play a chef on TV, and didn't want to look like a total dumbass when chopping vegetables. I enjoy "recreational cooking" though; it's something I've been fond of since I was a kid spending time in the kitchen with my parents, whether it'd be making banana bread from a *Sesame Street* book recipe with my mom, or improvising dinner with whatever seafood or pasta ingredients were around with my dad.

It was the 1990s when the original Japanese *Iron Chef* show came to America, one that a lot of people embraced for its originality during a time before food reality competition shows became all the rage. Inspired by the fancy food presentations in this show, I developed a game with my brother, Mark — "Iron Chef Buffet" — where we'd go to those all-you-can-eat Chinese buffets in suburbia, and try to outdo each other with the most artful presentation of a dish. Someone would come up with a specific category — soups, chicken, or desserts, for example — and we'd run out to the buffet and get as creative as possible with the available ingredients. My brother would hang shrimp off the side of his garnished egg drop soup, and I'd make a drizzle on a plate with chocolate icing from piece of sheet cake before laying down pastries and fruit. These food styling antics continued in my kitchen, and to this day, I try to make my ordinary food look better than it usually is, simply by dressing it up with fancy plates and garnishes — for no other reason than the fact that it amuses me.

The impetus to do this food styling hobby with *fast food* didn't come out of thin air; I've had a long history with fast food through the years. As a young child growing up in New Jersey in the 1980s, I sometimes attended birthday parties at the local McDonald's, where my fondess for the Golden Arches and Happy Meal toys was instilled in my young brain — just as they had planned! The brainwashing worked; as a teen, I often ate fast food when there weren't any home-cooked meals, or when I'd cruise around the area with friends when we got our driver's licenses and had nothing better to do. When I got older, I continued to enjoy fast food here and there — especially the day after a night of drinking or during a long road trip. I've also been known to have an occasional "Big Mac Attack."

Mind you, I wasn't eating fast food all the time; just enough for it to still be a part of my lifestyle — let it be known that my opinions of French fries, as well as fast food styling, have actually interfered with a couple of relationships I've been in. Fast food has also come into play at work in corporate America, where I once made Chicken McNugget tacos at my desk for my coworkers as a goof, with sixty Chicken McNuggets, an Old El Paso taco kit, and lettuce and tomatoes that I actually chopped by my workstation. Years later at the same firm, I competed in an unofficial company-wide eating contest where I scarfed down thirty Chicken McNuggets. (Although I accomplished this feat in 7 minutes and 16 seconds, I still came in last — the winner ate thirty McNuggets in an astounding 4 minutes and 32 seconds!)

My double life as a fast food consumer and an amateur food stylist came together when Facebook started going mainstream and I uploaded pictures of my home-prepared food creations to show off to online friends — only to be egged on by some of them who remembered my fast food past, with taunts like, "What, you're too good for fast food now?" At some point it clicked; an idea had incepted in my mind: *I should try to make fast food look fancy*. It was one of those ideas you get but don't really act on, however, it was something I kept in the back of my mind to do when I had an extra bit of time on my hands. That extra time fell into my lap in the spring of 2009, on an evening that I was supposed to get some exercise with friends — plans that had fallen through. In an ironic twist, I went to my local McDonald's instead, bought a Big Mac and fries, brought it to my kitchen, and converted it into a sliced steak and mashed potatoes dish served on a fancy white plate, accompanied by a small salad made from the strands of lettuce and mock croutons made out of the middle bun. I didn't actually eat all of this; I simply took pictures of it to post online for fun. A domain search showed me that "fancyfastfood.com" hadn't been registered yet(!), so I snatched it up right away, and the blog was born.

This act out of boredom eventually turned into a regular weekly hobby for me, right around the time that food blogs like This Is Why You're Fat were getting noticed. Also, the modern mainstream food revolution had already begun: the vilification of fast food and the gourmet renaissance. Living amongst foodies and "foodiots" in New York City, I noticed a lot of hypocrisy; people would rave about gourmet foods made with ingredients like pork belly or loaded with butter, but then shunned fast food, blaming it for making people obese. But didn't gourmet food, regardless of being more respected, also make you just as fat? And so, Fancy Fast Food became more than just a showcase of converting fast food to something that looks gourmet; it aimed to poke fun of food culture and its hypocrisy. As the tagline of the blog goes, "Yeah, it's still bad for you — but see how good it can look!"

On July 1st, 2009, after just five short weeks since I posted that first fancy Big Mac, FancyFastFood.com went viral in a single, magical day. It got a lot of online press, which led to radio press, which led to television press — not only in America but overseas: The Associated Press, *Time*, CNBC, *Guardian* (UK), Radio New Zealand, CBC News (Canada), *The National Post* (Canada), *Weekend Today* (Australia), *Sunrise* (Australia), France 24 News, The Smithsonian Institute, and most notably, *The New York Times*, where even acclaimed restaurant critic Frank Bruni wrote about it. I've done segments on ABC News' *Nightline*, the *Rachael Ray* show, and The Cooking Channel's *Food(ography)*, and had a hand in a fast food episode of Showtime's *Penn & Teller: Bullshit!* (I mean that literally; after three days of shooting interviews and a food experiment at Cornell University, the only thing that remained in the final edit was a quick B-roll shot of my hand.) Furthermore, Fancy Fast Food has been mentioned by Zagat, *Today*, CNN, and Comedy Central, in addition to being named one of the "Top Five Cool Food Sites" by Independent Film Channel's *Food Party*, *FHM*'s Website of the Week (July 2009), *InStyle* magazine's Best of the Web 2009, and *PC Magazine*'s Favorite Blogs 2009 and 2010. It has all led up to this book, *Fancy Fast Food: Ironic Recipes with No Bun Intended*, which might have been released sooner if not for being stuck for more than a year in publishing hell. To make a long story short, the book prevailed despite traveling on a much different publication path than originally planned. It's now in your hands — better late than never.

With everything that has happened with the blog, many just know me as "The Fancy Fast Food Guy." However, contrary to popular belief, I've actually cut down on my intake of fast food in recent years, and strive to eat fresher and healthier dishes — I even keep an indoor hydroponic organic garden in my apartment, or at least try to keep it from drying out. When I'm not playing with my food, I actually have better things to do (also contrary to popular belief): running a small company, writing for The Huffington Post and the Discovery Channel, and working as a freelance interactive and motion designer for several ad agencies in New York City. I also design T-shirts on CoverMyTorso.com (if you'll excuse the gratuitous plug). My other passion is international adventure travel, and I maintain an acclaimed travel blog, TheGlobalTrip.com (another plug) whenever I go abroad in search of new adventures — and new cuisines that don't necessarily involve fast food. However, fast food will always be a part of my life, just as it has been in the past. And no matter how little that may or may not be in the future, it's sure still going to be bad for me — but I'll definitely try and see how good it can look.

Photo: Phil Langer

ACKNOWLEDGMENTS

✲ ✲ ✲ ✲ ✲

It took a lot of hamburgers, chicken, burritos, pizzas, French fries and other greasy delicacies to produce this book over two years, but all that fast food might have remained plain and ordinary if not for the support of many people behind the scenes. It has been a long roller coaster of a ride for me to expand the Fancy Fast Food blog into my vision of a satirical cookbook, and a lot of that had to do with the persistence of my literary agent Paul Lucas, who manned the reins when I was thrown into this mysterious and confusing world of publishing. To make a long story short, this paperback edition exists after many, many long months of cooking, lighting, shooting, tasting, traveling, writing, editing, waiting, designing, rewriting, waiting some more, and arguing. A thank you goes out to editor Rachel Trusheim and her team for doing their part. Also, I owe a huge debt of gratitude to Maurice Murdock, not only for his continued support throughout the years, but for crafting the awesome illustrations in this book.

Although each mock recipe in this book was created by yours truly, there was typically someone assisting me on each one — whether it be giving me a ride to the restaurant (I don't have a car), helping me at the cutting board, lending me props or lights, doing research for backstory, or preventing the room from burning down when a lighting kit diffuser almost caught on fire this one time. I'd like to thank (in order of the recipes): Lana Price, Cheryl Triviño, Mark "Lingo" Laqui, Terence Rivada ("Wheat"), Stephanie Etkin (especially for our grand Middle American fast food road trip with Zoey), Dr. Brian Wansink and the crew at the Cornell University Food and Brand Lab (January 2010), Donatella Pereira, Devin O'Brien, Mitch Miller, my parents Ralph and Nata Trinidad (Here's my "good thing."), Noelle Royer, Jessica Bellamy, Ray Vazquez, ABC News correspondent Sharyn Alfonsi, *Bon Appetít* editor Andrew Knowlton, Kelly Buchanan, Chrissy Michaels, Jennifer Beninson ("Tucson, not Toussaint!"), Adam Lindsey, Robin Freni, Bill Massey, Kristen DeAngelis, Elaine Acosta ("This is better than the whale!"), Melissa Roach, Mark Utreras, Katy Garibay, Rachael Ray (our five-second conversation off camera was truly memorable, huh? "Ginny Lavish says hello."), Kirsten Teal, Cha Cha Leon, Jeff Wong, Kathy Chou Vargas, Sean Keener, my book mentor Lilit Marcus (we'll always have matzah brei), Jarrod Spillers, Deborah Basilio, Hans-Georg Basilio, Brigitte Basilio, Virginia Lopez, and Matt O'Grady.

Thanks also goes out to those who helped create the other Fancy Fast Food content and recipes not featured in this book: Adrian Fiorino (creator of the blog and book, Insanewiches), Sarah Donikian, Sarah Lim, Devon Knight and Jason Isch (of CornerstoreRestaurateur.com), Andrew Shapiro, Amy Schiller, Paul Goodman, Stacey Lavish, Beth McCabe ("Surprise!"), vegan chef and cookbook author Alexandra Jamieson, Phil Langer, Amanda Albergo, Megan Quinn, Susannah Masur, and the folks at NASA (when I attempted to make "Fancy Space Food") — Sara Mitchell, Maggie Masetti, Lynn Chandler, and Vickie Kloeris. Extra special thanks to my brother Mark Trinidad, who not only helped create "Doh-Mi-Noh Chow Mein," but has also been a tremendous one-man support team for all my projects throughout the years. If not for our "Iron Chef Buffet" battles, this book might have not come to be.

The hype and publicity of the Fancy Fast Food blog was also a big part of arriving at the publishing of this book. Thanks for the support from Hamilton Tamayo, George Northy, Rob Gomez, Sarah Lohman, Josh Ozersky, Faye Penn and the folks at Brokelyn, Erica Westly and *Wired*, Sarah Rosenberg and the crew of *Nightline*, Guy Bauer, Laurel Fantauzzo, Dan Delaney of VendrTV, Jessica Frankel Schutzman and the crews of *Rachael Ray* and *Food(ography)*, Jeff Potter (see page 7 of his book, *Cooking For Geeks*), Sara Bonisteel, Kat Kinsman, Cheryl Brown, Sarah DeHeer and AOL Slashfood, Anthony Layser, Jake Goodrich and Asylum/Masterclash, Babette Pepaj and Nichelle Stephens of BakeSpace and TechMunch, Eliot Glazer, Jessica Amason of This is Why You're Fat, Mike Barish, Meg Nesterov, Greta Peters, Alyson Hagert, Rachel (R.) Kelly, Colleen Williams, KK Rogne and the staff at Cowgirl, Kristin Sommers and the Zync crews at Ogilvy and American Express (Happy Festivus!), Emily Cavalier and my fellow food Tweeters, and everyone else who spread the word when the blog went viral, not only online, but on domestic and international radio and television.

I'd also like to acknowledge others not yet mentioned, who gave me additional support in some capacity: Gretta Krechmaras, Sal Barone, Marlies Gielissen, Laura Pence, Thomas Maher (Baja Fresh Challenge!) and the rest of my Organic friends who were there when this all started, Andrea Gerst, Scott Kawczynski, Ryan Dunlavey, Brandon Molloy, Cristina Frank, Jenny Cox, Michael DuDell, Emily Feinberg, Shea Kornblum, Aimee Trinidad (with

Logan and Mia), Andi Grossman, Natasha Rydowski, Lance Rydowski, The Fish Crew, Michael Rivera and all my relatives at John and Howard Streets, Melyssa Davis, John Schline, Teva Kukan, The Brooklyn Kitchen and Whisk for providing kitchen supplies nearby — plus whomever else I might have forgotten. Thanks also to Stephen Colbert and Jon Stewart (and all their writers), Dave Barry, Dan Carboni (R.I.P.), Mark Bittman, and Julia Child for comic and culinary inspiration.

I'd also like to give shout-outs to the fast food chains around the country that I've sourced my ingredients from (in order): Arby's, Burger King, Chick-fil-A, Five Guys, Domino's Pizza, White Castle, Schlotzsky's, KFC, Fuddruckers, Whataburger, Moe's Southwest Grill, Sonic, Zaxby's, McDonald's, Jack In The Box, Bojangles', Pizza Hut, Wendy's, In-N-Out Burger, Carl's Jr., Fatburger, Wienerschnitzel, Steak 'N Shake, Long John Silver's, Captain D's, Rubio's, Popeyes, Baja Fresh, Taco Bell, Del Taco, Checkers, Subway, Chipotle, Burgerville, Yoshinoya, Nathan's, 7-Eleven, Dunkin' Donuts, Culver's, Dairy Queen, Maggie Moo's, and Tim Hortons — plus all the other fast food chains that appear on the blog that hopefully can find the humor in all this. (The same goes to all the celebrity chefs I've poked fun of in this book as well.)

Indeed there have been a lot of people behind the scenes who unknowingly became a part of this satire on food culture, but it is not without them that this book came to exist. After all that has happened, I'm happy that it finally all came together — happier than a Happy Meal could ever be, even if it came with a really cool toy.

INDEX

✻ ✻ ✻ ✻ ✻

7-Eleven, 151, 180

A
Air-chilled, 73
Airline travel, 134
American, 2, 17, 25, 27, 39, 60, 75, 81, 86, 89, 92, 115, 118, 134, 141, 153, 158, 161, 167, 170, 178
American Domplings, 25-27
Anderson, Pamela, 167
Animal style, 76-78
Antibiotic-free, 73
Appetizers, 9-31
Apple pie, 43, 44, 61, 148, 150
Arby's, 10, 13, 180
Atkins dieters, 13

B
"Baby Got Back", 12
Baja Bouillabaisse, 111-112
Baja Fresh Mexican Grill, 111, 180
Banana, 17, 20, 50, 174
Banks, Tyra, 59
Batali, Mario, 5, 104, 106
Beans, 41, 42, 36, 47, 64, 66, 101, 104, 107, 110, 129, 142, 171
Beef, 10, 12, 13, 21, 23, 29, 42, 69, 75-85, 88-91, 93-94, 117-118, 125, 138, 140, 149
  bourgignon, 93-94
  C'Arbysccio, 10-11
  roast, 10, 12, 88
  Strog 'N Off, 89-90
  Wellington, Animal Style, 76-78
Beer, 66, 106, 126, 171
  Belgian, 79
  pong, 45
  root, 79-81
Belgium, 79
Bell, Glen, Jr., 118
Bento, 60-61
Biscuit, 15, 38, 42, 53, 64, 65, 107, 110
  with ham, egg & cheese, 14-15
BK (see Burger King)
Blintz, 161-162
Blitz (football), 161

Blizzard Blintz, 161-162
Bojangles', 64, 180
Borscht, (see Soup)
Boston Krème Brûlée, 156-157
Bouillabaisse, 111-112
Bourdain, Anthony, 17
Brangelina, 66
Brazil, 41
Bread, 6, 9, 13, 15, 18, 24, 31, 42, 44, 53, 56, 58, 61, 65, 78, 80, 86, 87, 90, 93, 100, 103, 126, 127, 142, 143, 152, 157, 166, 170, 174
Breakfast, 4, 15, 16, 39, 53, 149
Brown, Alton, 57
Bubbe Wendy's Hanukkah Latkes, 144-147
Bullock, Sandra, 101
Buns, 4, 13, 23, 24, 29, 31, 77, 93, 114, 123, 125, 142, 152, 160, 162
Burger King, 14, 16, 81, 82, 86, 92, 93, 148-150, 180
  Croissan'wich, 14, 15, 148, 149
  hash browns, 14, 15
  king, 16
  Quad Stackers, 149
  Steakhouse Burger, 93
  Whopper, 16, 51, 75, 93
Burgerville, 153, 180
Burrito, 6, 104, 106, 111, 112, 118-121, 129, 130, 173, 178

C
Cage-free, 3
Canada, 81, 167, 170, 176
Captain D's Seafood Kitchen, 101, 180
Carbon footprint, 3, 133, 134
Carbonade flamande, 79
Carlbonade Flamande, 79-81
Carolinas (North and South), 64
Carl's Jr., 79, 180
Carnivore, 13, 64, 135, 160, 166
Carrot cake, 166
Cartoons, 54, 60
Cassoulet, 46-47
Ceviche, 98-100
Cheat Potato Gnocchi, 133-135
Checkers, 123-125, 180
Cheerwine, 64-65
Cheese, 7, 12-14, 20, 25-31, 34, 42, 46, 51, 54, 56, 67, 69, 81, 83, 88-90, 123, 129-130, 134, 148-153, 161-162
Chef Boyardee, 117
Cherry
  limeade, 50
  picking, 158, 160
  popping, 158
  sundae topping, 161-162
Chick-fil-A, 17, 18, 180
Chick-Sat-A, 17-18
Chicken, 2, 3, 6, 12, 17, 18, 20, 25, 28-32, 36, 38, 39, 44, 52-73, 86, 87, 97, 107, 110, 111, 120, 126, 128-130, 135, 140, 143, 153, 173-175, 178
  Cheddar & Mushroom Zouffé, 54-56
  Chipotlioli, 129-131
  fingers, 56, 61, 67, 72, 87, 130, 153
  McConfit, Le, 57-59
  McNuggets, 52, 57-59, 175
  Mole Frostano, 70-72
  of the Sea, 107
  Pizza Masala, 67-69
  soufflé, 54
  wings, 67, 69, 72, 153
Child, Julia, 92, 94, 113, 179
Chili, 72, 128, 130, 138, 140-142, 160
Chinese, 25, 123, 125, 174
Chinese Checkers Chow Mein, 123-125
Chipotle Mexican Grill, 129
Chocolate, 66, 70, 72, 79, 167, 170, 174
Christianity, 18, 73

Christmas, 59, 148-150
Clams, 28, 29, 31, 112
Cock, 73, 97
Cocoa Puffs, 70
Coffee, 14, 16, 73, 167, 170, 171
Coleslaw, 38, 64, 66, 98, 100, 101, 103, 107, 110
Colonel's Chicken Corn Chowder, The, 36-39
Condiments, 21, 42, 46, 83, 104, 111, 112, 126, 129, 138
Confit, 57-58
Coq Au CheerVin, 64-66
Coriander, 67, 69
Corn, 3, 26, 38, 39, 45, 59, 83, 86-88, 98, 100, 141-143, 151
  chowder, 36, 38, 39
  dogs, 86, 87, 98, 141-143, 151
  as people, 39
  syrup, 3, 39
Cottage cheese, 89, 90
Crab, 97, 101, 103, 112
Cream, whipped, 35, 165
Crème brûlée, 156-157
Culver's, 158, 180
Culvoutis, 158
Cup size, 45
Cupid, 138

D
Da Vinci, Leonardo, 166
Dairy Queen, 161-162, 180
De Laurentiis, Giada, 95
Deen, Paula, 95
Del Spaghetti Arrabiatta, 120-121
Del Taco, 120, 122, 153, 180
Desserts, 48, 151-170, 178
Diarrhea, 2, 42
Disco fries (see New Jersey)
Discovery Channel, The, 2, 76, 176, 180
Domino's Pizza, 25, 27, 110, 180
Donuts, 156-157, 167, 170
Drive-thru, 9, 28, 51, 82
Drugs
  marijuana, 28-31
  roofies, 143

Dumplings, 25-26
Dunkin' Donuts, 156, 180

E
Eat Pray Love (film), 94
Eggs, 3, 15, 54, 88, 113, 163
Ells, Steve, 129

F
Fancy, 1-180
Farfalle (see Pasta)
Farting (see Flatulence)
Fat, 2, 21, 24, 41, 57, 58, 65, 79, 83, 85, 92, 97, 127, 136, 144, 160, 163, 173, 174, 176
Fatburger, 83, 85, 180
Feces, 130
Feijoada, 41
Filet-O-Fish (see McDonald's)
Fish (see Seafood)
Five-Dollar Farfalle, 126-127
Five-Dollar Footlong, 126
Five Guys, 21, 23
Five Guys Foie Gras, 21-23
Flatulence, 42
Flay, Bobby, 95
Fogle, Jared, 126-127
Foie gras, 6, 21-24
Fondue, 70, 145, 151-152
Fondue du Sept Onze, 151-153
Food movement spectrum, 12-13
Food processor, 27, 29, 56, 58, 65, 77, 78, 85, 87, 90, 93, 94, 125, 127-130, 145, 149, 157, 160, 162
Food porn, 5, 56, 174
Foodie, 5, 6, 76, 104, 133, 137, 176
Foodiot, 5, 176
Food(ography) (TV show), 46, 176, 179
Food Network, 137
Franksgiving Dinner, 141-143
Free-range, 3, 73
French, 6, 21, 46, 57, 68, 81, 83, 92, 113, 147, 156, 158
French fries, 2, 4, 6, 23, 28, 29, 57, 76, 79, 81-83, 93, 94, 141, 175, 178
  sweet potato fries, 82, 133, 134
Frosty (see Wendy's)
Fruit tart, 156-158
Fuddjoada, 41-42
Fuddruckers, 41, 180

G
Garnishes
  basil, 7, 34, 35, 120, 121, 128, 130
  chives, 7, 38, 54, 56-58, 143-145, 147
  cilantro, 7, 72, 104, 106, 111, 112
  coriander, 67, 69
  dill, 89
  effects on relationships, 7
  exception, 7, 173
  importance, 7
  lime zest, 51, 98, 100
  mint, 7, 156, 157, 165
  parsley, 7, 34, 35, 41, 42, 46, 47, 86, 87, 93, 94, 101, 103, 118, 119, 133, 134
  thyme, 7, 76, 78
Gazschlotzcho, 34-35
Gefilte fish, 115
Gnocchi, 133-135
Goose, 21, 24
Gras-Fed Steak Au Poivre, 83-85
Grass-fed, 3, 83
Gumbo, 101-103
Gumbo D-Luxe, 101-103

H
Halal, 73
Ham, 14, 15, 148-150, 173
Hamburger, 21, 23, 28, 39, 41, 42, 75, 76, 123, 133, 160-162, 173, 178
Hanukkah, 144, 145, 147
Harold & Kumar, 28
Hash browns, 14-15, 144-145
Haute cuisine, 6, 7
Hipsters, 13, 67
Honey Apple-Glazed Christmas Holiday Ham, 148-150
Hooters, 2
Horton, Tim (person), 167
Hot dogs, 6, 20, 72, 87, 122, 141, 142, 151, 152
Hot sauce (see Sauce)
Huey Lewis and the News, 5

I
Ice cream, 39, 50, 51, 70, 90, 162-165
Immigrant, 161
In-N-Out Burger, 76, 180
Indian, 143
Innuendo, 56
Iron Chef (TV show), 60, 61, 174
Islam (see Mohammed)
Italian, 123, 136, 167, 170

J
Jack in the Bento, 60-61
Jack in the Box, 60-61, 180
Jalapeños, 10, 13, 41-44, 120, 121
Japanese 3, 25, 60, 138, 140, 174
JELL-O, 166
Jenga, 149
Jesus Christ, 115, 150, 166
Judaism, 73, 115, 125, 144
Julie & Julia (film), 92

K
Kama Sutra (book), 67
Kentucky Fried Chicken (see KFC)
Ketchup, 28, 29, 31, 39, 76, 79, 80, 93, 113, 115, 120, 121
KFC, 2, 6, 36, 28, 81, 180
Kidney stones, 135
King of Quiche, 14-16
King, Martin Luther Jr., 151
Kitchen torch, 18, 20, 142, 145, 149, 157, 173
Kosher, 36, 73, 115
Kutcher, Ashton, 10
Kwanzaa, 137

L
Lachey, Nick, 107
Lagasse, Emeril, 95, 103
Lean Cuisiners, 13
Lee, Sandra, 95
Lemon juice, 98, 100
Leno, Jay, 59
Liposuction, 57
Lobster (see Seafood)
Locally sourced (food), 3, 133
Long John Ceviche, 98-100
Long John Silver's, 98, 100, 118, 180
Lord of the Rings (film), 45
Lunchlady (mean), 7

M
Mac & cheese, 7, 153
Maggie Moo's, 165
Maggie Mousse, 163-165
Maharajas, 2, 67, 69
Mahjong, 125
Masturbation, 110
McDonald's, 2, 3, 57, 58, 69, 81, 82, 113, 129, 144, 175, 180
  Big Mac, 69, 89, 153, 175, 176
  Chicken McNuggets, 52, 57-59, 175
  Filet-O-Fish, 51, 113, 115
  French fries, 2, 57, 82, 175
  Grimace, 129
  Hamburglar, 2
  Happy Meal, 2, 138, 175, 180
  McRib, 10
Menorah, 145, 147
Milkshake (also milk shake), 44, 83, 85, 89
Moe (illustrator) (see Murdock, Maurice)
Moe's Southwest Cassoulet, 46-47
Moe's Southwest Grill, 46, 180
Mohammed (prophet), 46
Moore, Demi, 10, 13
Mousse, 163, 165
Mr. Miyagi, 60
Mr. Roboto, 106
Munchies, 1, 28, 29, 31
Murdock, Maurice 46, 178
Mustard, 17, 21, 28, 57, 76, 79, 80, 149, 150
Myers, Mike, 167

N
Nachos, 151-152
Nathan's Famous, 141-142, 180
Neely, Pat and Geena, 95
New Jersey
  Bon Jovi, 28
  disco fries, 81
  fist-pumping, 28
  state, 2, 28, 81, 175
  Tony Soprano, 28
New Orleans, 101
New Year's, 151
New York City, 5, 43, 141, 176, 177
New York Observer, The, 5
New York Times, The, 66, 176
Nightline, 176, 179
Noid, The, 25, 27
Noodles, 87, 90, 117-134
NORAD, 36

O
Okra, 101, 103
Olive Garden, 9
Oliver, Jamie, 95, 179
Omnivores, 13
Onion rings, 28, 29, 31, 41, 42, 79, 80, 89, 90, 93
Oompa Loompas, 21
Organic, 3-5, 7, 12, 34, 38, 41, 46, 54, 57, 58, 67, 72, 73, 76, 86, 89, 93, 98

P
Paella, 138, 140
Paella Yoshinolla, 138-140
Pants, 113, 126, 127
Pasta, 90, 117-134, 174
  farfalle, 6, 117, 126-128
  ravioli, 25, 128, 130
  spaghetti, 117, 120-125
  tortellini, 116, 118, 119
Penn & Teller's Bullshit!, 38, 176
Pepper, 21, 25, 43, 44, 56, 64, 76, 83, 85, 93, 120, 122, 126, 128, 144, 145
PETA, 21
Pico de gallo (see Salsa)
Pilgrim, 45, 141-143
Pirate, 98, 98, 100
Pitt, Brad, 59
Pizza, 2, 4, 25-27, 66-69, 86,

94, 126, 153, 173, 178
Pizza Hut, 2, 67, 86, 180
Play-Doh, 117
Polish, 25, 50
Polo, Marco, 123
Pope, The, 115
Popeyes, 107, 180
Pork, 46, 47, 57, 64, 176
Poultry (see Chicken)
Poutine, 81
Presley, Elvis, 41
Produce (food), 31, 139, 160
Pyromania, 20 ,156

Q
Quad Stacker (see Burger King)
Quenelles, 113, 115
Quenelles-O-Fish, 113-115
Quiche, 14-16, 157

R
Rally's (see also Checkers), 123
Ramsay, Gordon, 163
Ravioli (see Pasta)
Raw foods movement, 10
Ray, Rachael, 95, 110, 176, 178, 179
Reality TV, 5, 73, 107, 174
Red velvet cake, 166
Reduction, 6
  cola, 31, 61, 110
  fruit punch, 12, 143
Ribs, 140
Rice, 61, 64, 66, 104, 106, 107, 110, 138, 140, 143
Risotto, 14, 106
Roast beef (see Beef)
Roberts, Julia, 94
Rocca, Mo, 46
Rubio's, 104, 106, 180
Russian, 50, 89, 161

S
Salad, 4, 5, 10, 12, 13, 17, 20, 39, 46, 47, 54-58, 61, 79, 81, 85, 93, 111, 113, 115, 133, 148, 150, 160, 175
Salsa
  cilantro & onion, 104
  Kaiser, 46-47
  pico de gallo, 41, 42, 111, 112
  tomatillo-red chili, 128, 130
Salt, 21, 26, 57, 64, 65, 76, 83, 85, 93, 104, 144, 145
Sanders, Colonel, 36
Satan, 20, 88
Satay, 18, 20
Saturday Night Live (TV show), 107
Sauce
  Arby's, 10, 13
  Asian Kick, 123, 125
  Ass Blaster, 122
  barbecue, 17, 57, 59
  Buffalo, 17, 53, 67, 153
  hot, 64, 65, 70, 72, 101, 103, 107, 110, 119-122
  Horsey, 10, 13
  Hot Mustard, 57, 148
  Polynesian, 17
  Sweet 'N Sour (also Sweet & Sour) 57, 59, 144-147
  Taco Bell's Border, 118, 122
  tartar, 28, 31, 97, 114
Schlotzsky's, 34, 35, 180
Schwarzenegger, Arnold, 14
Seafood, 97-115
  Fauxsotto, 104-106
  fish, 12, 51, 97, 98, 100-107, 112-115, 173, 179
  shrimp, 97-104, 106, 110-112, 140, 174
  lobster (also langostino lobster), 111-112
Seinfeld (TV show)
  "Soup Nazi" (episode), 43
  George Costanza, 66
  Kramer, 43
Seitan, 88
Shark Week, 97
Shichimi-Togarashi, 140
Shrimp (see Seafood)
Simpson, Jessica, 107
Sonic (America's Drive-thru), 48, 50, 51, 180
Soniccia, 48, 51
Soniccian Borscht, 48-51
Soufflé, 54, 56, 134
Sound of Music, The (film), 86
Soups, 32-51
  borscht, 48-51
  chowder, 36-39
  gazpatcho, 34
  stone, 33
  mulligatawny, 43-44
Sour cream, 50, 90, 104, 106, 120, 144, 145, 147
Southeast Asia, 17
Spaghetti (see Pasta)
Spam, 88
Spanish, 28, 35, 70, 112, 138, 140
Spicy Chicken Mocki Sushi, 107-110
Spurlock, Morgan, 2, 82
Starbucks, 171
Steak 'N Shake, 89, 90, 180
Steak Au Poivre, 83-85
Subway (restaurant), 126-127, 180
Sundaes (see Ice cream)
Super Mario Bros., 106
Sushi, 60, 61, 107, 110
Sustainability, 129, 133, 135
Sweet potato fries (see French fries)

T
Taco Bell, 86, 104, 106, 118, 119, 122, 180
Tacobellini, 118-119
Tacos, 46, 47, 86, 111, 112, 118, 153, 175 Tapas, 28-31
Tapas de Castillo Blanco, 28-31
Tex-Mex, 46
Texas
  state, 13, 43, 44, 54
  toast, 54, 56
Thanksgiving, 45, 141, 143
This Is Why You're Fat (blog), 176
Tim Hortons, 167, 180
Timbits, 167, 170
Tiramisu, 167, 171
Tiramisu di Timio, 167, 171
Tofu, 85, 165
Top Chef Masters (TV show), 7
Tortellini (see Pasta)
Tums (antacid), 138
Turkey legs, 142-143
TV dinner, 13, 60

V
Valentine's Day, 138, 140
Valentine's Paella Yoshinolla, 138-140
Vegans, 12, 88, 173
  raw, 10, 12
Vegetarians, 12, 74, 88, 135
  fake, 12
Venereal disease, 158
Vitaminwater, 93, 94

W
Wansink, Brian, 38, 178
Wendy's, 70, 72, 144, 145, 147, 180
  baked potato, 144, 145, 147
  Buttery Best Spread, 144, 145
  chili, 72
  Frosty, 70, 72
  hash browns, 144, 145
  mandarin oranges, 144
Whataburger, 43, 180
Whatagatawny, 43-44
When Harry Met Sally (film), 5
White Castle, 28, 29, 31, 140, 180
Whole Foods, 7
Whop Perguignon, 92-95
Whopper (see Burger King)
Wiener schnitzel, 86, 87
Wiener Schnitzel Fälschung, 86-87
Wienerschnitzel, 86-87, 180
Wikipedia, 25
Wonka, Willy, 21

Y
Yoshinoya, 138, 140, 180

Z
Zaxby's, 54, 180
Zucchini bread, 166

About The Author

Photo: Phil Langer

Erik R. Trinidad is a writer/designer who took his idea of "extreme makeovers" with fast food and evolved it into an international sensation; Fancy Fast Food has been featured on *Today*, *Women's Day*, *InStyle*, *FHM*, *Wired*, and *The New York Times*, and on television segments for *Nightline*, *Rachael Ray*, and The Cooking Channel's *Food(ography)*. Erik writes fast food reviews for The Huffington Post and adventure-related articles for the Discovery Channel. He lives in Brooklyn, New York.

www.ingramcontent.com/pod-product-compliance
Lightning Source LLC
Chambersburg PA
CBHW041539220426
43663CB00003B/80